C000156148

PROPAGATION

❖

DAVID SQUIRE

POCKET

GARDENING
GUIDES

PROPAGATION

❖

DAVID SQUIRE

Illustrated by Vana Haggerty

TIGER BOOKS INTERNATIONAL
LONDON

Designed and conceived by

THE BRIDGEWATER BOOK COMPANY LTD

Art Directed by PETER BRIDGEWATER

Designed by TERRY JEAVONS

Illustrated by VANA HAGGERTY FLS

Edited by MARGOT RICHARDSON

CLB 3375

This edition published in 1994 by

TIGER BOOKS INTERNATIONAL PLC, London

© 1994 Colour Library Books Ltd,

Godalming, Surrey

Printed and bound in Singapore

ISBN 1-85501-383-5

CONTENTS

ANCIENT CRAFT

❖

INCREASING numbers of plants is a desire few gardeners do not experience. One of the earliest plants to be regularly propagated was the grape-vine. Thousands of years ago the Egyptians grew vines and knew the technique of reproducing them.

GRAPE-VINES *have been cultivated for several thousand years, their fruits eaten fresh or made into wine. The leafy vines also created shade, much desired in hot, sunny countries.*

Later, the Romans, when extending their empire, spread vines throughout Europe, while centuries later grapes were introduced to North America and Australia, rivalling the best and longest-established vineyards in Europe.

OX DUNG
AND HORMONES!

In addition to being early viticulturists and propagators, the Romans experimented with encouraging the rapid development of roots. They dipped the bases of cuttings in ox dung to initiate the formation of roots, preceding the modern use of hormone rooting-powders by many centuries.

MOTHER
NATURE'S INFLUENCE

Many plants develop roots extremely easily. In earlier centuries when willow shoots were used to form fences they frequently produced roots. In the tropics and subtropics, screening plants root even faster: shoots of the Nicaraguan cocoa tree, when used to create shade in cocoa plantations in tropical America, soon develop roots in the moist soil and humid, warm weather.

Several methods of propagation utilize the natural inclinations of plants, and although often relatively slow are easily tackled by novice gardeners. Layering low-growing shoots and removing suckers from non-grafted or budded plants will, after a few years, produce plants like their parents.

The gardens of Rameses III in Ancient Egypt were tended by several thousand slaves. They were packed with grape-vines and fig trees increased from cuttings.

Many plants, when mature, shed seeds around themselves and create self-sown seedlings. These, too, offer simple ways to raise new plants, but remember that if the parent is an F.1 variety the seed it sheds will not produce replicas of the parent. F.1 varieties are created by crossing two pure bred, closely related varieties, producing plants that are more vigorous, larger and uniform than normal varieties. This has been of great benefit to home gardeners as well as nurserymen.

MAN'S INGENUITY

Shoots of one plant will sometimes naturally unite with others, but this is an exception. Gardeners, however, have created specialized forms of propagation by encouraging the buds or shoots of a selected variety to grow on root stocks of known vigour. Apples and pears are normally increased by grafting; most roses by budding techniques.

Many tropical and sub tropical plants are nowadays grown as houseplants in temperate countries. In part, this has become pos-

Many of the methods and techniques of propagation which the modern gardener uses today have been developed slowly over many centuries, by patient gardeners of the past.

sible because cuttings taken from the tips of plants produce short plants that flower at an early stage. Also, fruiting plants raised from young tip cuttings high up on a plant, both flower and produce fruits earlier than normal.

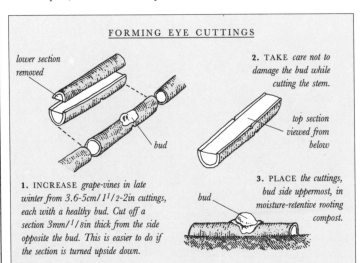

FORMING EYE CUTTINGS

lower section removed

bud

2. TAKE *care not to damage the bud while cutting the stem.*

top section viewed from below

1. INCREASE *grape-vines in late winter from 3.6-5cm/1^1/2-2in cuttings, each with a healthy bud. Cut off a section 3mm/^{1}/8in thick from the side opposite the bud. This is easier to do if the section is turned upside down.*

3. PLACE *the cuttings, bud side uppermost, in moisture-retentive rooting compost.*

bud

SIMPLE PROPAGATION

❖

THE range of plants that can be easily propagated is wide and includes annuals and biennials, vegetables, herbaceous perennials, cacti and other succulents, ornamental shrubs, houseplants and fruit bushes.

SIMPLE EQUIPMENT

The majority of plants can be increased without the need of specialized equipment. Some benefit from heated propagation cases in greenhouses or sunrooms, but often seeds germinate and cuttings develop roots quite easily in boxes and pots on window sills indoors.

Most vegetables, as well as annuals and biennials, are raised from seeds. Herbaceous perennials, although sometimes increased from seeds, are more frequently propagated by dividing established clumps in autumn or spring.

Ornamental shrubs are increased in many ways, including layering and cuttings. Most soft fruits, such as gooseberries, red currants and blackcurrants, are raised from cuttings.

A few plants grown as houseplants in temperate regions are increased in unusual and distinctive ways, such as by runners and plantlets, often to the amusement of children.

Fruit trees are increased by budding or grafting – a means of uniting a good fruiting variety with hardy roots. No special equipment is needed, other than a knife, raffia and grafting wax.

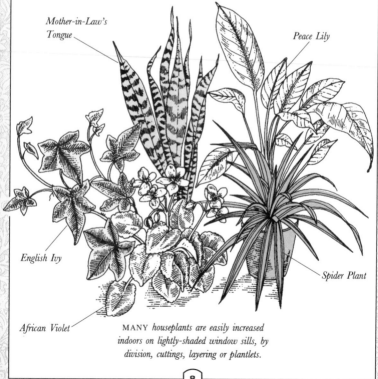

Mother-in-Law's Tongue

Peace Lily

English Ivy

Spider Plant

African Violet

MANY *houseplants are easily increased indoors on lightly-shaded window sills, by division, cuttings, layering or plantlets.*

EQUIPMENT AND COMPOSTS

❖

C LEAN equipment and com-
posts are essential. If pots,
seed-trays or boxes are dirty they
may contain disease spores from
the previous year, while contami-
nated compost soon decimates
seedlings and cuttings.

Wash all equipment in disinfec-
tant, rinse, allow to dry and let
fumes disperse before using.

COMPOSTS *are either soil- or peat-
based. Soil-based types are a mixture of
loam, sharp sand and peat, while peat
ones are mainly granulated peat.*

POTS *are needed in a range of sizes
for potting up established seedlings
and cuttings.*

UNHEATED
SEED-TRAYS
*with plastic lids
are an inexpensive
way to retain
warmth for
cuttings
and seed
germination.*

PLASTIC SEED-TRAY
*are ideal for seeds and
cuttings, as well as for
pricking out seedlings.*

HEATED
PROPAGATION *cases
enable seeds to be sown early
in the year, as well
as being a more assured
way to root soft-stemmed
cuttings.*

SHARP
KNIVES *are
essential when
preparing cuttings,
as well as for
budding and grafting.*

SHARP SECATEURS *are
useful when preparing
hardwood cuttings.*

SOWING SEEDS IN GREENHOUSES

HALF-HARDY annuals are sown in gentle warmth in greenhouses or sunrooms in late winter or spring. They are planted outdoors in the garden after all risk of frost has passed, then flower throughout summer. A few houseplants are also raised from seeds.

An advantage of increasing plants from seeds is that large numbers of them can be raised at one time.

REQUIREMENTS FOR GERMINATION

Whatever the type of plant, the seeds need three basic conditions to encourage germination: moisture, warmth and air. Most seeds germinate in darkness, but a few, such as the Wax Flower (*Begonia semperflorens*), need light.

Moisture is provided by sowing seeds in moisture-retentive peat- or loam-based compost. Soil from a garden is not suitable as it is likely to contain pests, diseases and weed seeds. Also, it usually has insufficient fertilizers and the wrong proportions of loam, peat and sand.

AFTER SOWING TREATMENT

The temperature and moisture in a compost are the main influences on germination. Air is also necessary, but if an open, well-drained compost has been used enough oxygen will reach the seeds.

Warmth is provided by placing a domed plastic lid or sheet of glass over the seed-tray. Electrically-heated propagation frames are another possibility, enabling seeds to be sown earlier in the year without having to warm up the entire greenhouse.

The precise temperature needed to initiate germination varies from one species to another. Check the instructions on the seed packet – usually between 16–21°C/61–70°F. Most seeds germinate in darkness. Therefore, cover the plastic dome or sheet of glass with newspaper until seedlings appear; then allow light in.

1. FILL *a clean seed-tray with seed compost and firm it, especially around the edges as these are the areas that inevitably dry out first if watering is neglected.*

2. ADD *further compost and use a straight-edged piece of wood to level it with the sides. Then, use a presser to firm the surface about 12mm/1/2in below the rim.*

3. TIP *seeds into a piece of stiff paper folded into a V-shape. Sprinkle a few seeds into it and sow them evenly and thinly by tapping the edge of the paper.*

4. TAKE *care not to sow seeds within 12mm/¹/₂in of the tray's sides. Most seeds germinate in darkness, so use a sieve to sprinkle compost over the surface.*

5. WATER *the compost by placing the seed-tray in a bowl of clean water until moisture seeps to the surface. Then, remove and allow excess water to drain.*

6. PLACE *a transparent lid over the seed-tray to help conserve warmth and to prevent the compost's surface drying out, harming the seeds and preventing germination.*

HELPING GERMINATION

Most seeds germinate within a few weeks, but some need help:

• Hard-coated seeds such as Sweet Peas and Morning Glory *(ipomoea)* resist the entry of moisture and air. Either gently rub the seed on sandpaper or carefully nick the coat with a sharp knife.

• Fluctuating temperatures help to break dormancy in seeds such as some lilies, tree paeonies and daphnes. Cold periods, followed by warm spells and then another cold period are often needed. Others need high night temperatures and low day ones. Specific instructions are usually detailed on seed packets.

• Cold periods also initiate germination. They make seeds of trees and shrubs believe winter has passed and spring has arrived. Initially, place seeds on moist blotting paper for a few days, then put in a sealed container in a refrigerator for a few months.

• Growth-inhibitor chemicals, present in some seeds, prevent rapid germination. Soaking in water leaches out chemicals, as well as softening them, and is ideal for cyclamen, *cytisus* (Broom), *caragana* (Pea Tree) and *clianthus* (Parrot's Bill).

F.1 HYBRIDS

These are produced by crossing two pure bred, closely related varieties. They are known as F.1 hybrids, which is short for 'first filial' generation. There are both vegetable and flowering F.1 varieties and most seed companies offer them in their catalogues.

Plants produced in this way are:

• *Larger and stronger than normal varieties.*

• *Uniform plants, creating a formal and unvarying appearance. This is ideal for summer-flowering bedding plants in formal arrangements, but does not create a cottage-garden display unless plants are placed at irregular intervals throughout a border.*

• *Uniformity in vegetable varieties has advantages and disadvantages. Plants are larger, but those raised from the same sowing tend to mature at the same time.*

Freezers help to utilize gluts; alternatively, make several sowings.

SOWING HARDY ANNUALS

❖

H ARDY annuals are traditional residents of gardens, sometimes in borders totally devoted to them or as fillers in herbaceous borders. Occasionally they are planted in mixed borders, where a wide spectrum of plant types are used to create variety.

Hardy annuals are nature's pace-setters: in one season they germinate from seeds sown outdoors, they develop stems and leaves and then they bear flowers that produce seeds before the onset of winter.

Half-hardy annuals, incidentally, are not so hardy and are sown in gentle warmth earlier in the year and planted into a border when all risk of frost has passed. They are also known as summer-flowering bedding plants.

CHOOSING THE SITE

If you have a large garden, there is a possibility of choosing a warm, weed-free, wind-sheltered place where the soil is fertile, well-drained but moisture retentive.

Often, however, it is more a matter of filling empty borders with colour. Nevertheless, digging the soil in winter, ensuring it is well drained and adding plenty of decomposed compost or manure is part of the recipe for success.

WHEN TO SOW

Sow hardy annuals from early to late spring, depending on the weather pattern in your area. In warm regions where frost is seldom experienced, seeds can be sown in early spring, but in other areas late spring or early summer are better. If you are new to an area, talk to knowledgeable neighbours – most gardeners are keen to air their knowledge about plants and the weather!

Birds and cats are often a nuisance: creating a network of black cotton 10-15cm/4-6in above the surface acts as a deterrent, although birds sometimes get underneath. Alternatively, place twiggy sticks over the sown area. Remove them when the seedlings

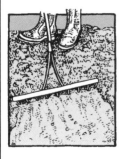

1. DIG *the soil in winter, leaving the surface rough but level so that by spring, frost, rain and wind will have reduced it to a fine tilth. In spring, use a large rake to break down lumps; level the surface and remove big stones.*

2. FIRM *the surface by systematically shuffling over the surface. This is the best way to consolidate soil evenly. Do not use a roller as invariably it is too heavy and if stopped, consolidates one area more than another.*

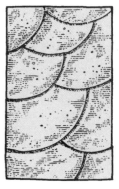

3. SKETCH *the border on graph paper and indicate the sowing areas. Then, transfer the plan to a border, using a pointed stick.*

are established and growing strongly. In dry weather, water the total area thoroughly but gently.

THINNING THE SEEDLINGS

When the seedlings are large enough to handle, thin them out, removing weak, sickly or damaged ones and leaving the others spaced apart equally. These spacings vary: whereas Love-lies-Bleeding (*Amaranthus caudatus*) seedlings are left about 38cm/15in apart, those of Love-in-a-Mist (*Nigella damascena*) need only be 15–23cm/6–9in. Check spacings on the seed packet. Thin the seedlings carefully and refirm those that remain, followed by a thorough but light watering. Seedlings left loosely in the ground soon become dry, and may die.

STAKING AND SUPPORTING

Immediately after thinning, insert twiggy sticks around plants so that they grow up and through them. Insert these sticks firmly in the ground and to a height slightly lower than each plant's predicted height – see seed packet.

CHILDREN IN THE GARDEN

From toddler to gardening enthusiast can be rapid and dramatic. When the novelty of repeated sand pies loses its fascination, children look for other gardening experiences and these often are sowing seeds.

The result of sowing seeds, however, has to be rapid and spectacular to retain their attention. Few annuals are better for this than Sunflowers, often the size of dinner plates, on plants 1.8m/6ft high and in rich, vibrant colours. Sown in their flowering positions in mid to late spring, they burst into flower in mid-summer.

Snapdragons are other fun plants and provide endless amusement for 'nipping' noses, while Foxgloves make tiny gloves for dolls and Nasturtium leaves form dolls' hats.

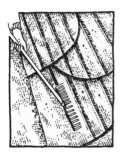

4. FORM *shallow drills 15–20cm/6–8in apart with the back of a garden rake. With experience, drills can be formed without using a straight-edged board or garden line. Draw hoes can also be used.*

5. SOW *seeds evenly and thinly. Do not sow them during windy weather or if the soil is very wet or dry. Do not feel obliged to sow the complete packet of seeds, as congested seedlings are susceptible to diseases.*

6. COVER *the seeds by shallowly using a garden rake. Do not disturb the seeds and avoid raking them out of the drill, as this makes weed identification difficult. Firm along the drill, using the rake's head.*

BIENNIALS AND HARDY HERBACEOUS PERENNIALS

Although they are different types of plants, biennials and hardy herbaceous perennials are both raised in seed-beds outdoors and later transplanted to their growing and flowering positions.

Biennials and hardy herbaceous perennials are sown in shallow drills in spring and early summer. When large enough to handle, thin the seedlings: these spacings vary according to a plant's stature and vigour.

The Daisy (*Bellis perennis*), a hardy perennial grown as a biennial, reaches only 10–15cm/4–6in high and is thinned 7.5–10cm/3–4in apart. Whereas Yarrow (*Achillea filipendula*), which grows up to 1.2m/4ft, is thinned to 30cm/12in. The hardy perennial Columbine (*Aquilegia*), growing 45–60cm/1¹/₂–2ft high, is thinned 15–20cm/6–8in apart.

The distances to which individual biennials and herbaceous perennials are thinned are usually indicated on seed packets.

TRANSPLANTING

In autumn of the same year, transplant young plants into their flowering positions, setting them slightly wider apart than when thinned out. Ensure that plants are firmly planted; in spring, re-firm those lifted by frost.

In extremely cold areas transplanting is sometimes left until early spring of the following year.

RAISING VEGETABLES IN SEED-BEDS

Several vegetables, such as cabbages, Brussels sprouts, cauliflowers and broccoli are initially raised in seed-beds and later transplanted to their growing positions. Asparagus seedlings and leeks are also raised in seed-beds. Established young plants, ready for transplanting, are frequently sold by garden centres and nurseries.

1. PREPARE *the soil in winter, digging the seed-bed, removing perennial weeds and mixing in decomposed compost and manure. In spring, use a large rake to level the surface, breaking it down to a fine tilth.*

2. FIRM *the surface by systematically shuffling over the surface. As well as consolidating the soil, shuffling helps to break down large lumps. Do not use a garden roller: it always makes the surface uneven.*

3. RAKE *the surface again and use a draw hoe to form shallow drills. A garden line or straight-edged board helps to create straight drills spaced 15-20cm/6-8in apart. Remove the garden line or board before sowing seeds.*

NATURAL INCLINATIONS

Some plants grown from seeds are raised in a different way from their natural inclinations.

ANNUALS *An annual is a plant that grows from seed, flowers and produces seeds within the same year. However, a few plants that are not strictly annuals are treated as such. For instance, Lobelia (Lobelia erinus) is a half-hardy perennial invariably grown as a half-hardy annual. Marvel of Peru (Mirabilis jalapa) is a perennial grown as a half-hardy annual, while Busy Lizzie (Impatiens walleriana) is a greenhouse perennial treated as a half-hardy annual.*

BIENNIALS *A biennial makes its initial growth one year and flowers the following one, then dying. However, several plants not strictly biennial are treated as such. For example, the Daisy (Bellis perennis) is a hardy perennial invariably grown as a biennial. Sweet William (Dianthus barbatus) is another perennial cultivated as a biennial.*

BIENNIALS RAISED FROM SEEDS

These include many plants that bring colour to borders in spring and early summer, such as:

- Canterbury Bell (*Campanula medium*)
- Foxglove (*Digitalis purpurea*)
- Hollyhock (*Alcea rosea/ Althaea rosea*)
- Honesty (*Lunaria annua*)
- Sweet William (*Dianthus barbatus*)
- Wallflower (*Cheiranthus cheiri*)

HERBACEOUS PERENNIALS RAISED FROM SEEDS

- Anchusa (*Anchusa azurea*)
- Bee Balm (*Monarda didyma*)
- Columbine (*Aquilegia vulgaris*)
- Cupid's Dart (*Catananche caerulea*)
- Fleabane (*Erigeron speciosus*)
- Incarvillea (*Incarvillea delavayi*)
- Sea Holly (*Eryngium maritimum*)
- Shasta Daisy/Max Daisy (*Chrysanthemum maximum*)
- Valerian (*Centranthus ruber*)
- Yarrow (*Achillea filipendula*)

 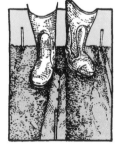 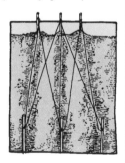

4. SOW *seeds evenly and thinly in shallow drills, taking care not to drop them in clusters. Congested seedlings are susceptible to diseases, as well as creating unnecessary competition for water, air and nutrients.*

5. COVER *the seeds by straddling the row and shuffling along, directing soil over them. Alternatively, use a garden rake. Afterwards, firm soil over the seeds either with your feet or the top of a garden rake.*

6. RAKE *lightly over the surface – in the direction of the drills – to remove feet marks and depressions. This prevents rain water resting in puddles on the surface. If birds are a nuisance, cover with wire netting or sticks.*

SOWING VEGETABLES

◆

MOST vegetables are raised from seeds sown in V-shaped drills or, in a few cases, in flat-bottomed trenches.

V-SHAPED DRILLS
Use a draw hoe to form these drills. Their depths, of course, need to be related to the seeds and their sizes. The depths of drills for a range of vegetables are:
• 12mm/^{1}/$_2$in: Chicory, Endive, Leeks, Lettuce, Onions, Salsify.
• 12–18mm/^{1}/$_2$–^{3}/$_4$in: Asparagus, Carrots, Kohlrabi, Marrows, Parsnips, Radishes, Spinach, Squashes, Swedes, Turnips.
• 18–25mm/^{3}/$_4$–1in: Broccoli, Brussels sprouts, Cabbages, Cauliflowers, Kale.
• 25mm/1in: Asparagus peas, Beetroot, Sweet corn.
• 5cm/2in: Garden Peas, Beans – French, Runner, Haricot, Soya.
• 7.5cm/3in: Broad beans
• 15cm/6in: Jerusalem artichokes and Potatoes.

IN TRENCHES
A few vegetables, such as peas, are sown in flat-bottomed trenches. They can also be sown in V-shaped drills, but to produce more peas from a similar sized area they they are best sown in 20–23cm/8–9in wide and 5–6.5cm/2–2^1/$_2$in deep, flat-based trenches.

Sow seeds in three rows, 7.5cm/3in apart and the seeds similarly spaced within the rows. Stagger the seeds in the centre row so that they 'have the maximum amount of space. Spacing out seeds in this way helps to reduce the amount of seed needed, as well as eliminating the need to thin out seedlings later.

CONTINUOUS LINES
Most vegetable seeds are sown thinly and evenly in continuous lines in drills. After germination and when large enough to handle, the seedlings are thinned out to the desired spacings. It is therefore a waste of seed and money to sow seeds thickly.

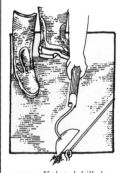

FORM *V-shaped drills by using a draw hoe. Use a garden line to ensure the row is straight and walk backwards using the hoe. If the row is long, stand on the line to prevent it being moved sideways.*

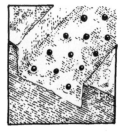

FLAT-BOTTOMED *trenches are formed either with a draw hoe or spade: 20–23cm/8–9in wide and 5–6.5cm/2– 2^1/$_2$in deep. Sow peas in three rows, 7.5cm/3in apart and a similar distance in rows.*

SOW SEEDS *evenly and thinly in a single line along the base of a V-drill. Ensure seeds are spaced out, as if they are congested it encourages unnecessary competition for light, air, moisture and nutrients.*

IN CLUSTERS

Instead of sowing seeds in continuous trickles in drills, vegetables such as parsnips are sown in groups of three or four seeds spaced 10–15cm/4–6in apart. After germination and when the seedlings are large enough to handle, they are thinned to leave the strongest at each position.

THINNING SEEDLINGS

When seedlings are large enough to handle they can be thinned. Leaving this task too long results in thin, leggy and weak seedlings.

Unless the soil is already moist, lightly but thoroughly water the soil during the previous day.

Usually, seedlings are thinned in two stages; first to half the ultimate distance, later to the full spacing. This ensures that should a seedling die after the first thinning, the maximum gap left between them will only be one-and-a-half times the full spacing, not twice the distance.

Carefully pull up unwanted seedlings, taking care to re-firm those that have been loosened. Afterwards, lightly but thoroughly water the seedlings.

KEEPING SEEDS

Inevitably, by mid-summer gardeners are left with opened seed packets partly filled with seeds. But what to do with them and do they 'store' well?
- *All seeds progressively lose their ability to germinate the longer they are kept, although this widely varies from one species to another. Most seeds remain viable for at least two years, but parsnip seeds rapidly lose their ability to germinate immediately the seed packet is opened. For such vegetables, buy only small packets of seeds.*
- *Store seeds in their packets or paper bags, sealing the tops to prevent moisture entering. Do not place them in plastic bags or polythene containers as this retains any moisture that might be present.*
- *Place them in a dry, cool place where the temperature remains constant and low, or in a refrigerator. Label packets.*

SOW *some seeds, such as parsnips, in small groups. After germination, remove the weakest seedlings, leaving only the strongest. This ensures that the remaining seedlings are at the desired and optimum spacings.*

THIN *seedlings as soon as they are large enough to handle. Re-firm the remaining seedlings and thoroughly but lightly water them. Pick up unwanted seedlings; leaving them on the soil encourages pests and diseases.*

FLUID SOWING *is when seeds are mixed with a fluid gel such as wallpaper paste and squeezed out into the base of a drill. It helps to retain moisture around seeds and encourages rapid and even germination.*

SOFT-WOOD CUTTINGS

Rooting soft-wood cuttings is a popular and easy way to increase soft-stemmed plants. These include many plants grown as houseplants in temperate climates, as well as dahlias and chrysanthemums that are raised in greenhouses early in the year and planted outdoors as soon as all risk of frost has passed.

CHRYSANTHEMUMS AND DAHLIAS

These popular plants frequently grow more than 1.2m/4ft high and have stems that harden and become slightly woody as the season progresses. In late winter and spring, however, they can be increased from soft-wood cuttings.

Roots (known as stools) are dug up in autumn, stems cut down to about 15cm/6in high and packed in boxes with clean soil around them. In late winter or spring – after being watered and placed in gentle warmth – the stems will

HORMONE ROOTING-POWDERS

These have been used for many years to encourage the development of roots. The bottom ends of cuttings are dipped in rooting-powder and inserted in compost.

This encourages cuttings to develop roots quickly, which helps to diminish the time when they are vulnerable to decay. Also, most hormone rooting-powders include fungicides that further help to reduce the risk of diseases entering cuttings.

Rather than dipping the cuttings directly into a tin of hormone rooting-powder, tip some into a lid and dip the bases of cuttings into it. This prevents all the powder being ruined if the cuttings are exceptionally moist and drip water over it.

Store the powder in a dry place. In damp places, put the container in a large screw-top jar.

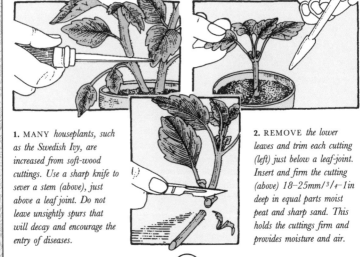

1. MANY *houseplants, such as the Swedish Ivy, are increased from soft-wood cuttings. Use a sharp knife to sever a stem (above), just above a leaf joint. Do not leave unsightly spurs that will decay and encourage the entry of diseases.*

2. REMOVE *the lower leaves and trim each cutting (left) just below a leaf-joint. Insert and firm the cutting (above) 18–25mm/³⁄₄–1in deep in equal parts moist peat and sharp sand. This holds the cuttings firm and provides moisture and air.*

duce soft shoots that when 10–15cm/4–6in long can be formed into 6–7.5cm/2^{1}/$_{2}$–3in long cuttings.

These are prepared by cutting beneath a leaf joint and removing the lower leaves. Then, insert them about 2.5cm/1in deep in equal parts moist peat and sharp sand. Water gently to settle compost around their bases.

PLASTIC BAGS

Cuttings are encouraged to root by placing them in plastic bags or propagation units.

Some units are unheated, while others are warmed by electricity. However, a popular and inexpensive way to create a warm, humid atmosphere is to place a plastic bag over them. It should not touch the leaves or stems: therefore first insert four or five thin canes in the compost. Draw a plastic bag over them and secure to the pot with an elastic band.

Regularly check the cuttings to ensure they are not touching the bag. Pot up when rooted.

MIST-PROPAGATION

Until recently, only commercial mist-propagation units were available, but ones for enthusiastic amateurs are now widely sold.

Mist propagation units are electrically operated and designed to automatically maintain a thin film of water droplets over the cuttings. This keeps them cool and prevents leaves wilting while the bases of their stems are forming roots.

The compost in which the cuttings are inserted is warmed by electricity cables and this further encourages the rapid development of roots.

ROOTING CUTTINGS IN WATER

Encouraging soft-stemmed cuttings to root by suspending their stems in water delights children as well as producing new plants.

Busy Lizzie (Impatiens walleriana) *readily develops roots: prepare each cutting by severing the stem just below a leaf joint and removing the lower leaves. Fill a glass or milk bottle to within 2.5cm/1in of the top with clean water. Place a piece of card over the container's top and pierce a hole in it so that the stem passes through but is held firmly. The lower 2.5cm/1in of stem should be in the water.*

Position the glass or bottle on a warm, lightly shaded window sill. Take care not to let the water-level fall as it then allows roots that have formed to dry out. When rooted, pot up and place in light shade until established.

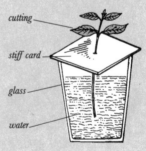

cutting

stiff card

glass

water

The white-edged Swedish Ivy (Plectranthus coleoides 'Marginatus') *is an easily grown houseplant. It creates colour and interest throughout the year.*

HALF-RIPE CUTTINGS

◆

THESE are also known as semi-mature and semi-hardwood cuttings, and are formed of shoots more mature than soft-wood types but not as old and tough as hard-wood ones.

Half-ripe cuttings are taken from 10–13cm/4–5in long shoots during mid-summer and into the early part of late summer.

PREPARING CUTTINGS

Shoots with 'heels' have their lower leaves removed and the heel slightly trimmed, removing whisker-like pieces from their edges. Normal half-ripe cuttings also have their lower leaves removed, but their bases are cut to just below a leaf joint.

Heathers are increased from cuttings only 6–7.5cm/2^1/$_2$–3in long, usually with heels of older wood attached to their bases.

INSERTING CUTTINGS

Insert the cuttings – three in a 7.5cm/3in-wide pot or five in a 13cm/5in one – to about one-third of their length in equal parts moist peat and sharp sand, after having dipped their bases in a hormone rooting-powder.

Place in a cool, sun-sheltered garden frame or under a cloche. Alternatively, they often develop roots when placed against a warm but sunless wall – but this is not recommended for cold areas.

Rooting is not rapid and usually it is not until spring of the following year that they can be planted into a nurserybed in a sheltered, lightly shaded corner of your garden. Ensure that their roots do not dry out. Later they are moved to their permanent positions. Do not set them in a border until they are well established.

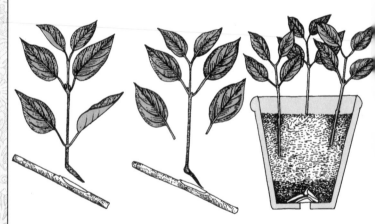

1. TAKE *half-ripe cuttings during mid-summer when shoots are firmer than for soft-wood types. Remove 10–13cm/4–5in long shoots, preferably with a piece of older wood still attached to their bases.*

2. REMOVE *the lower leaves and trim the cutting's base, cutting off whisker-like growths from around the heel. These heels – formed of older wood – are not essential, but they encourage rapid rooting.*

3. DIP *the base of each cutting in hormone rooting-powder and insert 3.6–5cm/ 1^1/$_2$–2in deep in equal parts moist peat and sharp sand. Firm compost around the cuttings. Then, water the compost thoroughly.*

HARDWOOD CUTTINGS

THESE are taken mainly from early to late autumn from mature shoots of the current season's growth. In theory, hardwood cuttings can be taken from autumn to early spring, whenever plants are dormant, but usually it is an autumnal task.

Some hardwood cuttings are taken with 'heels', but by far the most are not. These cuttings are variable in length, from 15–38cm/ 6–15in but the vast majority are 23–30cm/ 9–12in.

PREPARING HARDWOOD CUTTINGS

Use sharp secateurs to cut their bases slightly below a bud. If the top of a cutting is green and immature, cut it back to just above a healthy, mature bud.

Most hardwood cuttings are taken from deciduous plants and therefore by the time shoots are formed into cuttings they are bare of leaves. If, however, semi-evergreen plants are increased in this way, remove the lower leaves.

INSERTING HARDWOOD CUTTINGS

In a sheltered, out-of-the-way and well-drained part of a garden, form a 15–20cm/6–8in deep drill with one vertical side. Place sharp sand in its base and position the cuttings along the vertical side. Firm soil around them.

In spring, re-firm the soil, as it is likely to have been loosened by winter frost. Use the heel of your shoe to firm the soil.

These cuttings take about a year to develop roots. Then they are moved to wider spacings in a nurserybed until large enough to be given permanent positions.

1. SELECT *healthy, mature, pest- and disease-free shoots produced during the current season. Their lengths vary according to the species, but usually they are 23–30cm/ 9–12in.*

2. REMOVE *lower leaves and trim beneath a leaf joint. Most plants increased by hardwood cuttings are deciduous, but some, like the Privet shown here, are partially evergreen.*

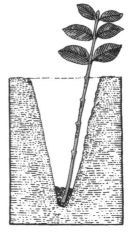

3. FORM *a trench with one vertical side and place a handful of sharp sand in its base. Insert cuttings to about half their lengths and firm soil around them, using your shoe to ensure firmness.*

ROOT CUTTINGS

❖

SOME plants can be increased by cutting up their roots and encouraging these to develop roots. It enables many new plants to be raised from a single parent.

Root cuttings are used to increase many herbaceous perennials, as well as a few shrubs with fleshy roots. Some shrubs, however, that are candidates for being increased by root cuttings, also develop sucker-like growths and frequently it is easier to increase them by that method (see pages 52 and 53). The Staghorn Sumach (*Rhus typhina*) is an example of this dual role.

The thickness of roots varies from one species to another: those about 12mm/¹/₂in thick are inserted vertically, while thinner ones are laid horizontally on to moisture-retentive compost.

All of the roots must be free from diseases and pest damage.

Do not take root cuttings from the roots of budded or grafted plants, as they will not produce replicas of the varietal part.

PLANTS INCREASED FROM THIN-ROOT CUTTINGS
- Drumstick Primrose (*Primula denticulata*)
- Perennial Phlox (*Phlox paniculata*)

PLANTS INCREASED FROM THICK-ROOT CUTTINGS
- Anchusa (*Anchusa azurea*)
- Californian Tree Poppy (*Romneya coulteri*)
- Cupid's Dart (*Catananche caerulea*)
- Mullien (*Verbascum*)
- Oriental Poppy (*Papaver orientale*)
- Sea Holly/Eryngo (*Eryngium*)
- Staghorn Sumach (*Rhus typhina*)

THIN-ROOT CUTTINGS

1. LIFT *plants during their dormant periods, in autumn and winter. An alternative to lifting an entire plant is to expose a few roots and to sever them. Wash the roots to remove soil and to make preparing them easier.*

2. CUT *thin roots into pieces 3.6–7.5cm/1¹/₂–3in long and lay them on the surface of equal parts moist peat and sharp sand to which has been added a dusting of more sand to increase aeration and drainage.*

3. COVER *the roots with a 12mm/¹/₂in layer of equal parts sharp sand and peat. The surface of the compost should be 12–25mm/1¹/₂–1in below the seed-tray's top. Lightly but thoroughly water the compost to settle it around the roots.*

THICK-ROOT CUTTINGS

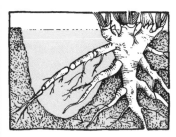

1. LIFT *or expose (above) the roots of plants with thick roots in the same way as for thin types. Sever the roots into pieces 6–7.5cm/2¹/₂–3in long. Make a flat cut at the end nearest the plant's centre, and a slope at the other end.*

2. INSERT *the cuttings, slant-side downwards, in equal parts moist peat and sharp sand. Press the top flush with the compost and add a 12mm/¹/₂in layer of equal parts sharp sand and peat. Lightly but thoroughly water the compost to settle it around the roots.*

AFTERCARE

After root cuttings have developed roots they are best planted into a nurserybed until large enough to be transferred to their permanent positions in a garden.

However, if they are small, instead of planting them directly into a nurserybed, first pot them up into loam-based compost in small pots. Keep the compost moist and place in a cool position.

AERIAL ROOTS
IN TROPICS

In warm, humid regions, some trees produce aerial roots that grow downwards, fix themselves in the soil and develop roots. They then either support the parent tree, prolonging its life, or are severed and encouraged to become independent plants.

On a smaller scale, several houseplants native to warm regions develop aerial roots. These include philodendrons and monsteras. They, too, have roots that sprawl and frequently trail around the plant's base.

Man's influence

In Sri Lanka (former Ceylon), aerial roots of certain rubber plants were encouraged to reach the ground and develop roots. Long canes of a giant bamboo, with stems up to 15m/50ft high and more than 13cm/5in in diameter, were split lengthways and the inner part removed.

The two parts were then placed around an aerial root and tied together in several places.

The lower end was securely fixed in the ground, while the upper one had moss tightly packed around the stem to prevent vermin such as rats and squirrels entering the bamboo tunnel and damaging the root.

After the aerial root had developed normal roots, it was severed from the parent and transplanted to its permanent growing position.

In recent years, with the introduction of propagation frames with controlled warmth and humidity, many of these traditional and tropical ways to increase plants have ceased. However easy and clinical modern methods are, they do not have the mystique and country-craft fascination of techniques used in earlier years.

LEAF-STEM CUTTINGS

◆

THIS is an excellent way to increase plants with long stems that are packed with small leaves. It is frequently used to reproduce climbing and trailing houseplants grown for their attractive foliage, such as the many attractively variegated ivies.

Increasing plants by leaf-stem cuttings has the benefit of enabling one long stem to produce many cuttings. Specimen plants are therefore not decimated and their appearance spoiled, especially if only a single stem is cut from the plant's back.

PLANTS INCREASED FROM LEAF-STEM CUTTINGS
• Canary Island Ivy (*Hedera canariensis* 'Gloire de Marengo': also known as 'Variegata')
• English Ivy (*Hedera helix* – including the many varieties with attractive leaves, such as 'Glacier', 'Jubilee', 'White Kolibri', 'New Sicilia', 'Pittsburgh', 'Chicago', 'Gold Child', 'Little Diamond', 'Sagittaefolia', 'Eva' and 'Anne Marie')
• German Ivy (*Senecio mikanioides*)
• Wax Ivy/Cape Ivy (*Senecio macroglossus* 'Variegatus')

1. CUT *a long, young, healthy stem from a parent plant, severing it either at the plant's base or close to a leaf joint. Do not leave unsightly spurs.*

2. USE *a sharp knife to cut the shoot into several cuttings. Cut slightly above each leaf joint, leaving a handle-like piece of stem 36mm/1¹/₂in long.*

3. USE *a small dibber to form a hole 18–30mm/³/₄–1¹/₄in deep in equal parts moist peat and sharp sand. Firm the compost around each cutting.*

4. WATER *the cuttings. Insert split canes at the edges, draw a plastic bag over them and secure it with an elastic band.*

5. PLACE *in light shade and gentle warmth. When young shoots appear at the leaf joints, remove the bag and give them fresh air.*

6. POT UP *rooted cuttings. Put one, three or five cuttings in each pot – a high number creates an attractively bushy plant quickly.*

LEAF-PETIOLE CUTTINGS

THIS is a novel but practical way to increase plants, and frequently used to propagate African Violets *(Saintpaulia ionantha)*. It enables a single mother plant to create many new ones. Petiole is the botanical term for leaf stem.

CREATING LEAF-PETIOLE CUTTINGS

These can be taken throughout the year, but spring and early summer are the best times.

Their preparation is easy and involves trimming the stem to about 36mm/1¹/₂in long. It is then inserted in equal parts moist peat and sharp sand, leaving the leaf blade resting slightly above the surface. The leaves of African violets are soft and hairy, and must not become wet.

ROOTING AFRICAN VIOLETS IN WATER

This technique seldom fails to fascinate children.
- *Fill a small bottle to within 18mm/³/₄in of its top with clean water. Wrap a piece of paper over the bottle's top and secure it around the rim with string or an elastic band.*
- *Carefully pierce the paper so that the stem when pushed through fits snugly, and its base is 12mm/¹/₂in in the water.*
- *Check the water regularly to ensure the stem's base is covered.*
- *After roots have formed, pot up into individual pots.*

1. USE *a sharp knife (above) to sever the stems of leaf-stalks close to the mother plant's base. Avoid leaving short spurs, as these encourage the onset of decay and presence of diseases. Choose healthy leaves that have not been damaged by pests or diseases, or burned by strong sunlight.*

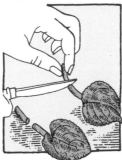

2. TRIM *the stem to 36mm/1¹/₂in long. Dip the end in hormone rooting-powder and, using a small dibber, insert and firm each stem 2.5cm/1in deep (above). Gently water. Insert split canes into the compost and cover with a plastic bag.*

WHOLE-LEAF CUTTINGS

❖

SEVERAL large-leaved plants grown in greenhouses and homes can be increased by placing a leaf flat on damp compost to encourage the formation of roots and new, healthy plants.

Use only leaves that are healthy and representative of the species. Do not use those that are old, or through neglect have dried and withered edges – they never produce vigorous, attractive plants.

When severing leaves from a mother plant, take them from several sides so that the plant's shape does not become imbalanced.

MOTHER PLANT
The day before cutting the leaves, water the mother plant thoroughly to ensure that its leaves are full of moisture. Wilting leaves do not create good cuttings and seldom root satisfactorily.

Leaves can be encouraged to form new plants throughout the year, but spring and summer are the best times as mother plants are usually healthier. Also, leaves

root quicker when the light is strong and plentiful.

Take care not to place the leaves in high temperatures or strong, direct sunlight. A north-facing window sill indoors, or a shaded greenhouse bench, is much better than scorching heat – a constant day temperature of 15–18°C/59–64°F is desirable. High temperatures dry the compost and desiccate leaves.

PLACING ON DAMP COMPOST
Leaves are selected, stalks removed, veins severed and the whole leaf laid flat on damp compost formed of equal parts moist peat and sharp sand. Secure them to the compost with U-shaped pieces of wire or small pebbles. Cover with a transparent lid and place out of direct sunlight. Check the compost regularly and if dry, stand the seed-tray in a bowl shallowly filled with water, until moisture seeps to the surface. Remove and allow excess water to drain.

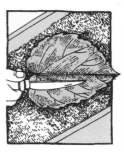

1. USE *a sharp knife to sever the stem of a leaf close to the plant's base. Do not leave short spurs at the base as they look unsightly. Try not to spoil the plant's shape: select leaves from around the complete plant.*

2. TURN *the leaf upside down and sever the stalk. Then, make several cuts, 18–25mm/³/₄–1in apart, through the main and secondary veins. Try not to cut through the whole leaf, as it then might fall apart.*

3. PLACE *the leaf – vein-side downwards – on equal parts moist peat and sharp sand. Use small pieces of bent wire to secure the leaf to the compost. It must be in close contact with the soil.*

4. ALTERNATIVELY, *place small stones on top of the leaf and around its edges. The disadvantage of this method is that shoots, as they grow, may be obstructed. However, if the leaf is regularly checked they can be quickly removed.*

5. PLACE *the seed-tray in a bowl shallowly filled with water. Remove it when the surface is damp, and allow excess water to drain away. Cover the seed-tray with a transparent lid. Regularly wipe off condensation from the inside of the lid.*

6. WHEN *young plants develop on the leaf's surface, carefully remove them and pot up into individual pots of potting compost. Water the compost and place the plant in gentle warmth and light shade until established. Avoid strong sunlight.*

POTTING UP

When roots have formed and shoots developed from the leaf's surface, carefully detach each young plant and pot up individually in a potting compost. Water and keep shaded until established.

Take care when potting up young plants: they should not be put in too large pots. When small plants are in large pots it is difficult to keep the moisture content in the compost just right. It usually becomes too wet and subsequently too cold. Under these conditions, plants soon decay.

PLANTS INCREASED FROM WHOLE-LEAF CUTTINGS

Iron Cross Begonia (*Begonia masoniana*) is a distinctive large-leaved begonia, ideal as a centre-piece on a coffee or dining room table. The lop-sided, somewhat heart-shaped, crinkled-surfaced, mid-green leaves have four or five deep bronze bars radiating from their centres.

Rex Begonia (*Begonia rex*), also known as King Begonia and Painted-leaf Begonia, dislays colourful, variedly patterned leaves and is ideal for decorating tables. In winter, place on a north-facing window sill, but in summer avoid direct sunlight.

Cape Primrose (*Streptocarpus x hybridus*) has long, spoon-like, corrugated, mid-green leaves and a wealth of trumpet-shaped flowers on long stems from late spring to late summer. These flowers include shades of red and purple, as well as white. It is ideal for decorating cool, lightly-shaded rooms in summer.

*The Rex Begonia (*Begonia rex*) is a superb houseplant, creating a dominant feature throughout the year. Placing it in a white cache pot highlights the attractive leaves.*

LEAF SQUARES
AND LEAF TRIANGLES

HESE are both ways to increase large-leaved begonias, and from one healthy leaf it is possible to produce eight or more new plants.

Healthy, relatively young leaves, free from pests and diseases, create the best cuttings. And ensure the compost is moist before severing them from the parent plant. Indeed, it is best to thoroughly water the compost several times during the preceding week, and to position it out of direct sunlight.

Dry, shrivelled leaves never produce strong, fast-rooting cuttings. A reserve of moisture within each cutting is essential.

CREATING CUTTINGS
From spring to mid-summer is the best time to take and root these cuttings. Use a sharp knife to sever the stalk close to the leaf. Turn the leaf over so that it is the right way up, and with a sharp knife form triangles. The apex of each cutting must be towards the centre, where the stalk originated. Always use a sharp knife as ragged cuts take longer to heal and produce roots.

INSERTING CUTTINGS
Fill a seed-tray with equal parts moist peat and sharp sand, and firm it to within about 12mm/ $^1/_2$in of the top.

LEAF SQUARES

These are used similarly to leaf triangles – but are square. Earlier, the squares were more popular than triangles, but now are not so fashionable. This is because:

- *It is easier to insert triangles into the compost and to get them to stand upright.*
- *There is less chance of triangles falling over when initially watered.*
- *Leaf squares are smaller than the triangles and therefore do not contain such as large reserve of food and moisture.*
- *It is easier to ensure that the cuttings are inserted the right way up.*

1. USE *a sharp knife to cut a leaf-stalk close to the plant's base. Do not leave short, unsightly pieces of stem on the mother plant as these decay and encourage the presence of diseases.*

2. TURN *the leaf upside down and cut off the leaf-stalk close to the blade. The leaf must be healthy and turgid: if dry and shrivelled it will not readily produce healthy roots.*

3. PLACE *the leaf – the top side uppermost – on a flat board and use a sharp knife to form triangles. The tip of the triangle must always be in the leaf's centre, from where the stem originates.*

Use a knife or thin spatula to form holes 18–25mm/ 3/4–1in deep in rows in the compost. Insert each cutting point down: hold its top, place in a hole and firm compost around its base. After insertion, the cuttings should not touch each other.

Lightly water the compost to settle it around the cuttings. However, take care not to water them excessively as this may disturb them from the best rooting position.

Insert a label in the seed-tray, indicating the date of planting and the plant's name.

Place a translucent plastic lid over the seed-tray, and position it in gentle warmth and a lightly shaded position. Avoid high temperatures and direct sunlight, as this soon dries the compost and shrivels the cuttings. Indeed, successful rooting is more likely on a cooler east or north-facing window sill than a southerly one in strong sunlight.

Periodically, wipe away condensation from the inside of the

Iron Cross Begonia (Begonia masoniana) is ideal for decorating tabletops in cool rooms.

translucent lid. If left, it drips on the cuttings and causes the onset of decay.

Regularly check the compost to ensure it is moist. Water by standing the the entire seed-tray in a bowl shallowly filled with water. When moisture percolates to the surface, remove the seed-tray and allow excess water to drain.

Do not water leaf cuttings from above, as moisture then remains on their surfaces and encourages them to decay. Leaves are usually at more risk than stems from decay caused by water.

POTTING UP

Rooting is indicated when shoots appear from the bases of the cuttings. Pot them up individually – the small leaf still intact – in small pots of potting compost. The leaf will eventually decay and fall off.

After potting, water gently and place in light shade until established and the young plant is growing strongly.

4. INSERT *the cuttings, pointed ends downward and to about half their lengths, in equal parts moist peat and sharp sand. Firm compost around them, then carefully and lightly water.*

5. COVER *with a translucent lid. Periodically, check compost; if dry, stand the tray in water until the surface is damp. Avoid wetting the leaves as they may decay.*

6. WHEN *rooted, pot up into a small pot of potting compost; water and place in gentle warmth.*

CROSS-SECTIONS OF LEAVES

SOME plants are reproduced by cutting their leaves crosswise into strips about 5cm/2in deep. They are then inserted in moisture-retentive but well-drained compost, watered and placed in gentle warmth.

PREPARING CUTTINGS

Water the plants several times during the few days before taking the cuttings. Dry leaves never root quickly and soon die.

Choose healthy and relatively young leaves that are good examples of the species.

Use a sharp knife to sever them at their bases. Do not leave small stubs of leaves as they are unsightly and eventually will decay.

Place the leaves on a clean board and use a sharp knife or scalpel to cut them into 5cm/2in-wide strips. Take care not to mix up the pieces as it is essential that the side nearest to the leaf stalk is inserted into the compost.

When inserting leaves of Mother-in-Law's Tongue, allow their surfaces to dry for a day before insertion – it encourages more rapid rooting.

1. SELECT *a healthy, relatively young leaf and cut it off close to its base. Take care not to spoil the plant's shape by removing too many leaves at one time or by taking them from the same position. The leaves are tough and therefore the knife must be sharp.*

2. CUT *the leaf into cross-sections about 5cm/2in deep. Use a sharp knife or scalpel and avoid tearing the edges. Ensure that the sections are not turned upside down, as each piece is inserted with its lower end downwards.*

3. FILL *and firm a pot with equal parts moist peat and sharp sand. Spread a thin layer of sharp sand over the surface. Use a knife to make slits in the compost to insert them 18mm/³/₄in deep. Firm compost around each cutting. Lightly but thoroughly water the compost from above.*

Mother-in-Law's Tongue (Sansevieria trifasciata) is an eye-catching plant with upright, sword-like, dark green leaves displaying transverse bands mottled light grey.

INSERTING CUTTINGS

Fill a seed-tray or pot with equal parts moist peat and sharp sand. Sprinkling sharp sand on the surface encourages greater aeration around the cuttings and induces faster rooting.

Use a knife or spatula to form slits in the compost into which the cuttings can be inserted 18mm/³/₄in deep. Firm compost around their bases.

Lightly water the compost to settle it around the cuttings, taking care not to disturb them. Avoid watering them too heavily.

After all moisture has dried from the leaves, either cover with a translucent plastic dome or place in a propagation frame.

Gentle warmth encourages root development, but do not expose them to high temperatures. Indeed, a gently warm but shaded, north or east-facing window sill is better than a southerly one in full sun. Cuttings soon become brittle and dry in strong sunlight and high temperatures.

Periodically, remove the cover and wipe away condensation. Also, check the compost and if dry, stand the pot or seed-tray in a shallow bowl of water until moisture rises to the surface. Then, remove and allow to drain.

When young shoots develop, pot up the cuttings into individual pots. Water the compost and place in gentle warmth and shade until established. Then, reduce the temperature and place the young plants in light shade.

*Cape Primrose (*Streptocarpus hybridus*) creates red, purple or white, foxglove-like flowers from late spring.*

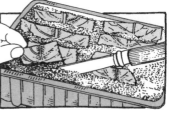

2. FILL *and firm a seed-tray with equal parts moist peat and sharp sand. Use a knife to form slits and insert the cuttings 18mm/³/₄in deep. Ensure they are upright.*

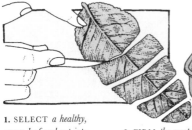

1. SELECT *a healthy, young leaf and cut into 5cm/2in-wide sections. Leaves taken from dry plants do not readily develop roots, so water the compost during the previous day.*

3. FIRM *the compost around the cuttings. Water lightly but thoroughly to settle compost around their bases. Place in a propagation frame or cover with a translucent lid. Avoid moistening the leaves as this encourages decay.*

CANE CUTTINGS

❖

Cane cuttings are formed from stems and resemble thick cuttings. They are frequently created from the stems of plants that have lost their lower leaves.

Cutting up a main stem clearly destroys a plant, however tatty it may appear through the loss of its lower leaves. However, each stem can be used to create several new plants, so the original plant is not entirely wasted.

Spring and summer are the best times to form cane cuttings, as once rooted they have time to establish themselves before the onset of cold winter weather.

There are two types of cane cuttings: those laid flat on moist compost, and the ones that are inserted vertically. Horizontal cuttings usually root quicker than tougher vertical ones.

VERTICAL CANE CUTTINGS

After a few years, yuccas invariably lose their lower leaves and although these plants have a distinctive and 'architectural' appearance they eventually outgrow available space indoors.

Chop up the stems into 7.5–10cm/3–4in long pieces – but

1. INCREASE *yuccas by forming vertical cane cuttings. Cut or scrape away wax (if present) from the lower end, but leave it on the top part.*

2. FILL *a pot with equal parts moist peat and sharp sand and insert the lower 36–50mm/1¹/₂–2in of the cutting. Firm the compost, water and allow excess to drain.*

3. PLACE *the pot in an opaque bag and position in gentle warmth. Inspect the compost every ten days to ensure it is moist. Water as necessary. When shoots appear, remove the bag and slowly acclimatize the plant to a lower temperature.*

Placing the plant in a plastic bag both increases the temperature and humidity, but the compost must remain moist at all times.

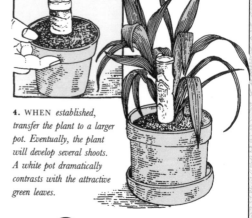

4. WHEN *established, transfer the plant to a larger pot. Eventually, the plant will develop several shoots. A white pot dramatically contrasts with the attractive green leaves.*

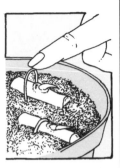

1. DUMB *canes are increased from cane cuttings during spring and early summer. Use a sharp knife to sever healthy stems at their bases, but try not to spoil the plant's shape.*

2. USE *a sharp knife to cut a stem into 5–7.5cm/ 2–3in lengths, each piece having at least one strong and healthy bud. These buds grow from the old leaf joints.*

3. FILL *a pot with equal parts moist peat and sharp sand. Position the stems, bud-side upwards, and secure with bent wires. Cover with a plastic bag and place in gentle warmth.*

take care to remember which are the tops and bottoms of the canes. These are then inserted 36–50mm/1¹⁄₂–2in deep in equal parts moist peat and sharp sand.

Place in an opaque bag and position in gentle warmth. Regularly check the compost to ensure it is moist. Remove the bag when shoots appear and slowly acclimatise the rooted cutting to a lower temperature and less humidity. Later, it can be transferred to a larger pot.

HORIZONTAL CANE CUTTINGS

Dumb Canes, dracaenas and cordylines are increased from cane cuttings laid flat on damp compost. Sever a strong and healthy stem from a mother plant and cut it into 5–7.5cm/2–3in long pieces, each with at least one bud.

Push each cutting into a mixture of equal parts moist peat and sharp sand. Secure the cuttings in the compost with bent wires.

Water lightly, allow surplus to drain and cover with a plastic dome. Alternatively, insert four or five small split canes in the com-

post, and close to the pot's edge, then draw a transparent plastic bag over and secure around the pot with an elastic band. Place in gentle warmth, and when rooted remove the covering and decrease the temperature. When established, transfer to a larger pot.

PLANTS INCREASED FROM CANE CUTTINGS
• Cordylines
• Dracaenas
• Dumb Cane (*Dieffenbachia*)
• Yuccas

HOLIDAY GIFTS

Frequently, when holidaying in warm countries, Ti-log cuttings are sold as gifts to take home. Cuttings from Brazil are sold as Lucky Plants and usually have their ends sealed with paraffin wax to prevent desiccation.

The top of each cane is indicated by a specific colour. This ensures the cuttings are inserted into the compost the right way up.

CACTI AND
OTHER SUCCULENTS

AS WELL as being grown from seed, many cacti and other succulents can be propagated from cuttings taken during spring and summer.

Cacti with clusters of small stems are easily increased by severing them at their bases. Water the plant during the previous day and use a sharp knife to sever stems. Ensure short, unsightly stubs are not left on the mother plant. Wear gloves to prevent spines damaging your hands.

Allow the cut surfaces to dry for a couple of days before inserting them about 12mm/¹/₂in deep in equal parts moist peat and sharp grit, with a surface covering of sharp sand.

Water lightly but thoroughly to settle compost around the cuttings and place them in gentle warmth. Make sure they are away from direct sunlight.

INCREASING SUCCULENTS

Many succulents are easily increased from cuttings. The Jade Plant (*Crassula argentea*) has fleshy leaves that can be inserted vertically into well-drained and aerated compost, while the October Plant (*Sedum sieboldii*) has flat, coin-like leaves that are laid flat on the surface of compost.

Like cacti cuttings, they must be taken from well-watered plants and the cut surfaces allowed to dry for several days before insertion in compost.

When inserting cuttings, do not place them within 12mm/¹/₂in of the container's sides as this is where the compost first becomes dry if watering is neglected.

Place the cuttings in gentle warmth and light shade. Check the compost regularly to ensure it is moist – stand the pot in a tray of water if necessary.

1. CACTI *with small stems can be increased in spring and summer. Select a young, healthy plant and with a sharp knife cut stems at their bases. Stems taken from around the outside of a clump root quicker than old ones at the plant's centre.*

2. LEAVE *the cuttings exposed to the air for a few days. This encourages them to root faster than if inserted immediately after being severed. Take care not to remove the cuttings just from one part of the mother plant.*

3. FILL *and firm a small pot with equal parts moist peat and sharp grit, then add a sprinkling of sharp sand over the surface. Use a small dibber to form a 12mm/ ¹/₂in deep hole and insert and firm the cutting.*

CACTI OR SUCCULENT?

There is often confusion about these widely used terms:

• Both cacti and succulents are succulent plants because of their ability to store water, but not all succulents are cacti.

• Cacti belong exclusively to the Cactaceae family and are distinguished by having areoles (resembling small pincushions) from which spines or long and woolly hairs grow. Flowers and stems also develop from the areoles.

• All cacti, with the exception of Pereskias – a group native to the New World and known as Leaf Cactus – do not bear leaves.

• Cacti are divided into two general groups: desert types whose natural environment is warm, semi-desert regions in the American continent, while forest types come from tropical America. Forest cacti are recognised by their trailing habit. They include the Christmas Cactus (*Schlumbergera truncata*, also known as the Crab or Claw Cactus), and *Schlumbergera russelliana*.

CIRCULAR LEAVES

 Succulent plants such as the October Plant (Sedum sieboldii) are increased by pulling off mature leaves, allowing the surfaces to dry for a couple of days and then pressing them flat on well-drained and aerated compost, such as equal parts moist peat and sharp sand with a thin surface layer of sand. Lightly water and place in gentle warmth in light shade.

The variegated form (Sedum sieboldii 'Medio-variegatum'), with cream and blush-green leaves, is increased in the same way, and is a much more attractive form for growing indoors.

1. SUCCULENTS *such as some crassulas and echeverias can be increased from entire leaves. Select a well watered plant and gently pull off mature, fleshy leaves, close to the stem. Do not leave short spurs on the mother plant.*

2. ALLOW *the cut surfaces to dry for a couple of days before inserting them in well-drained and aerated potting compost, formed of equal parts moist peat and grit, with a surface layer of sharp sand.*

3. WATER *the compost to settle it around the cuttings, and place in gentle warmth but away from direct sunlight. When shoots appear from their bases, gently pot them individually into sandy potting compost.*

DIVIDING HERBACEOUS PERENNIALS

❖

HERBACEOUS plants survive in cold regions because during autumn and early winter they die down to ground level and are perpetuated in the soil as dormant roots. In spring, they develop shoots and stems that later in the season produce flowers. In autumn, plants again die down.

AUTUMN OR SPRING?

Divide herbaceous plants any time between early autumn and mid-spring, whenever the weather and soil are suitable. Usually, this means in autumn where the weather is mild, but in spring in areas where cold winters are regularly experienced.

First, cut all stems to within a few inches of the ground. Clear away all debris, including weeds, and use a garden fork to dig up the clump.

If the clump is removed from the border and put on a lawn or path, first place sacking underneath. To divide small clumps, either lever the pieces apart with two hand forks placed back-to-back and their handles pulled together, or just with your hands. Large, woody and matted clumps are separated with two garden forks inserted back to back and levered together.

Discard old, central parts and retain only young pieces from around the outside. If roots are extremely matted, wash them in water and use a label or small, pointed stick to comb them out.

Replant the new pieces before their roots become dry. If this is impossible, wrap them in moist sacking and place in a cool shed. But plant them as soon as possible before their roots suffer.

Preferably, water the soil a few days before setting new plants in the ground: if planted in dry soil they will immediately lose moisture and may die.

If the divided plants are extremely small, they are best planted into a nurserybed for one or two years before setting them in a border. Also, if they are slightly tender, plant them in pots and place in a cold frame until large enough to be set in their permanent places in a garden.

1. FIBROUS *rooted herbaceous perennials when congested are easily increased. Use a garden fork to lift a matted clump. Place on sacking to prevent soil making paths or grass dirty.*

2. GENTLY *pull the clump into small but good-sized pieces. Discard central, old and woody parts and retain only those from around the outside. Pieces from around the edges are the youngest.*

3. MATTED *roots are sometimes so entangled that a knife is needed to separate them. However, usually they can be pulled apart by hand. Replant the pieces as soon as possible. Firm the soil.*

TYPES OF HERBACEOUS PLANTS

There are several types of herbaceous plants, their growth and roots influencing the ways in which they are increased:

<u>Plants with fibrous</u>, spreading roots are easily increased by lifting whole plants and gently dividing them (see base of previous page). Suitable plants include:

- Artemisias
- Asters (including the autumn-flowering Michaelmas Daisy as well as summer-flowering types)
- Bee Balm *(Monarda didyma)*
- Coneflower *(Rudbeckia fulgida)*
- Golden Rod *(Solidago)*
- Herbaceous campanulas
- Herbaceous geraniums
- Herbaceous phloxes
- Loosestrife *(Lysimachia punctata)*
- Masterwort *(Astrantia)*
- Meadowsweet *(Filipendula)*
- Pearl Everlasting *(Anaphalis)*
- Perennial Spiraea *(Astilbe)*
- Perennial Sunflowers *(Helianthus decapetalus)*
- Purple Loosestrife *(Lythrum)*
- Shasta or Max Daisy *(Chrysanthemum maximum)*
- Sneezewort *(Helenium)*
- Tickseed *(Coreopsis)*
- Yarrow *(Achillea)*

<u>Plants with fleshy roots</u> and woody crowns are increased by lifting the plant and using a sharp knife to separate the crowns. Plants include:

- Delphiniums
- Lupins *(Lupinus polyphyllus)*

<u>Plants with rhizomatous roots</u> are frequently grown in herbaceous borders. Their division is detailed on page 38.

- London Flag or Fleur-d-Lis *(Iris germanica)*
- Oris Root

DIVIDING LARGE, TOUGH CLUMPS

Neglected borders frequently have large clumps of herbaceous plants that have matted roots and masses of stems. Their centres are frequently very woody.

INSERT *two garden forks back to back (above) in a large clump and lever their handles together (right). This pulls them apart and disentangles their roots. This technique may need to be carried out several times before a clump is in small pieces. Do not use a spade as this invariably damages the roots, as well as the shoots.*

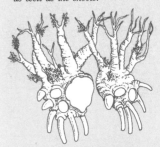

USE *a sharp knife to separate woody crowns of herbaceous plants such as delphiniums and lupins. Ensure that each new piece has strong roots and several growth buds.*

DIVIDING RHIZOMES AND TUBERS

❖

PLANTS with rhizomes or tubers are readily propagated by dividing. These food storage organs enable them to survive winter, live from one season to another and develops flowers quickly.

There are several types of irises: some bulbous and diminutive and including *Iris reticulata* and the honey-scented *Iris danfordiae*, both flowering in late winter and early spring. Other irises are bigger, more dominant and develop rhizomatous roots that securely anchor them in the ground.

The Fleur-de-lis or London Flag Iris (*Iris germanica*) is a rhizomatous type, with fleshy, tough and thick, concertina-like roots that often protrude above the surface. Such plants are easily increased after their flowers fade in early summer, or alternatively in late summer.

Clumps soon become congested, and lifting and dividing them every three years ensures that the flower quality does not diminish.

FLEUR-DE-LIS

Stories abound about this famous iris. In the twelfth century, Louis VII of France in his crusade against the Saracens adopted irises into his heraldry. Initially they were known as Fleur de Louis, corrupted into Fleur de Luce and later to Fleur de Lys and Fleur de Lis.

Lily-of-the-Valley (*Convallaria majalis*) has slender rhizomes. Lift plants with a garden fork at any time from late autumn to early spring and divide them.

Gently pull them apart and replant individual crowns just below the surface with about 10cm/4in between them.

These highly-scented, late spring and early summer-flowering plants are frequently planted

1. SOME *irises have thick, fleshy root-stems known as rhizomes – slightly buried or, with age, partly on the surface. After flowering, dig up the plants gently.*

2. DIVIDE *clumps, carefully selecting young pieces from the outside. Discard old, central parts. A sharp knife is essential. Each piece must have one or two fans of leaves.*

3. REPLANT *the rhizomes, either in a nurserybed or directly into a flower border. Tops of young rhizomes should be just level with the soil's surface.*

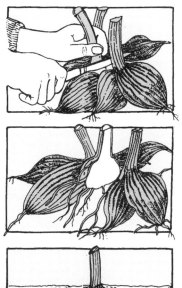

1. DAHLIAS *develop swollen roots known as tubers. In autumn, dig them up, cut off the stems and store in a cool, dry shed. In mid-to late spring, use a sharp knife to divide the tubers - each new plant must contain a stem because dahlia tubers do not contain buds.*

2. PLANTS *that have grown vigorously during the previous year often have congested tubers but only a few stems. Such plants can have their stems cut vertically with a sharp knife, but ensure each new stem has at least one healthy bud.*

3. AFTER *division, dust cut surfaces with a fungicide to prevent the entry of diseases. Plant the new plants about 15cm/6in deep. If practical, insert strong stakes first. If stakes are inserted later there is the possibility of them piercing tubers.*

alongside house walls – but take care as when congested they disturb brickwork.

DIVIDING DAHLIAS

Bedding dahlias are usually raised from seeds, but border types are increased from cuttings or division of the tubers.

Division is the easiest and simplest method and does not need specialized equipment. It is essential, however, that tubers are lifted in late summer or early autumn and stored in a frost-proof shed during winter.

DAZZLING DAHLIAS

The first European to describe the dazzling Mexican dahlias and their medicinal qualities was Francisco Hernandez, the sixteenth-century physician and botanist to Philip II of Spain.

In 1789, Vincent Cervantes of the Botanic Gardens in Mexico City sent dahlia seeds to the Royal Gardens in Madrid, where they germinated and developed a rich medley of flowers.

At this stage, by the way, it was thought that the tubers were edible, like those of the potato, another American plant.

Dahlias spread to France and the Empress Josephine grew them in her world-famous garden at Malmaison, near Paris. Dahlias sent from Spain to England in the 1790s failed to establish themselves and it was plants from Malmaison that eventually introduced dahlias to England.

Dahlias also became popular in Germany, where they became known as *Georgine*, after the Russian botanist Georgi of St Petersburg.

DIVIDING HOUSEPLANTS

THIS is the easiest and quickest way to create new houseplants. And as long as mother plants are not divided into too small pieces, the new plants immediately look attractive.

Any plant with masses of stems is suitable for division. Often, houseplants such as ivies, Peace Lilies and Mind-your-own-Business are grown and sold with several small plants in the same pot. This enables nurserymen to produce marketable plants earlier than if only one plant was put in each pot. This invariably produces a plant that when congested with foliage can be divided into several separate plants.

The day before dividing a plant, thoroughly water the compost. Remove the pot by inverting the plant, placing a hand under the root-ball and tapping the pot's rim on a firm surface. If the roots are very matted and congested, pass a knife between the soil-ball and the inside of the pot.

Gently pull the roots apart to produce several good-sized and attractive plants, each with as much root as possible. Do not break the plant into a lot of pieces that do not look attractive.

REPOTTING

Select a clean pot that size-wise is in balance with the plant to be set in it. Apart from small plants in large pots appearing imbalanced, it is difficult to keep the moisture content of the compost right when a plant's roots do not fill at least half of it. The compost often then becomes too wet and cold to encourage root development.

Fill the base of a pot with compost and position the plant to check its depth. Set the plant fractionally lower than before – to allow for subsequent settlement of the compost – and ensure a space about 12mm/^{1}/$_2$in is left between the compost's surface and rim. This enables the plant to be watered. If a small space is left, the plants are not properly watered.

1. DIVIDE *congested plants with masses of stems, such as Peace Lilies, by first removing the pot. Invert the pot, place one hand under it and tap the edge on a firm surface. The soil-ball will separate from the pot.*

2. GENTLY *pull the roots and stems into several pieces, each formed of several shoots. Do not try and create a large number of plants: it is better to form two or three good-sized plants than five or more sparsely-leaved ones.*

3. POT *up each new plant. Place potting compost in the pot's base and hold the plant in the centre. Trickle compost around its roots, ensuring the plant's depth is slightly lower than before. Firm compost to 12mm/^{1}/$_2$in below the top.*

1. DIVIDE *plants with a few stems, such as Mother-in-Law's Tongue by removing the pot and gently pulling the root-ball into several pieces. Do not divide it into too small pieces which may look unattractive.*

2. SELECT *a clean pot, add a small amount of compost, place a plant on top and adjust its height so that its level is the same as before. Ensure the roots are well spread out and not congested in one place.*

3. FILL *the pot with compost and firm it around the roots, leaving 12mm/ ¹/₂in between the compost and pot's rim. Water the compost and place in gentle warmth and light shade until established.*

Spread out the roots, then trickle and firm compost around them. Carefully water the compost to settle it around the roots. Use a rose on the end of a watering-can to avoid compost being unduly disturbed around the roots.

Place the plant in a warm, slightly shaded position until established and growing strongly.

As well as being increased by leaf-petiole cuttings, African Violets can be propagated by dividing congested plants. Old specimens are often formed of several small plants. In spring or summer, remove the plant from the pot and gently separate into several pieces. Discard old pieces and pot up the youngest.

HOUSEPLANTS INCREASED BY DIVISION

- African Violet
  (*Saintpaulia ionantha*)
- Aspidistra/Bar-room Plant
  (*Aspidistra elatior*)
- Bead Plant (*Nertera depressa*)
- Buffalo Grass
  (*Stenotaphrum secundatum*
  'Variegatum')
- Common Ivy
  (*Hedera helix* – and its many
  varieties)
- Ferns – many can be divided
- Japanese Sedge
  (*Carex morrowii* 'Variegata')
- Mind-your-own-Business
  (*Soleirolia soleirolii*)
- Never Never Plant
  (*Ctenanthe oppenheimiana tricolor*)
- Palms – some can be divided
- Peace Lily (*Spathiphyllum wallisii*)
- Peacock Plant
  (*Calathea makoyana*)
- Prayer Plant
  (*Maranta leuconeura*)
- Selaginellas
- Spider Plant
  (*Chlorophytum comosum*)
- Sweet Flag (*Acorus gramineus*)

LAYERING PLANTS OUTDOORS

◆

AYERING is an easy way to increase garden plants and does not need specialised equipment. Shoots and stems are left attached to parent plants and severed after roots form. They are then transferred to a nurserybed or a border.

LAYERING SHRUBS

Shrubs with low-growing stems – as well as trees with pendulous branches – are easily increased by layers. It can be performed at any time throughout the year but late summer to early autumn, as well as spring, are best. Essentially, shoots must be pliable so that they can be lowered to the ground.

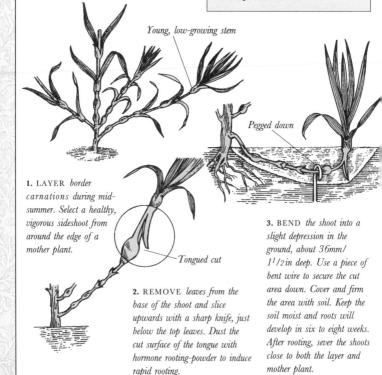

Young, low-growing stem

Pegged down

1. LAYER *border carnations during mid-summer. Select a healthy, vigorous sideshoot from around the edge of a mother plant.*

Tongued cut

2. REMOVE *leaves from the base of the shoot and slice upwards with a sharp knife, just below the top leaves. Dust the cut surface of the tongue with hormone rooting-powder to induce rapid rooting.*

3. BEND *the shoot into a slight depression in the ground, about 36mm/ 1¹/₂in deep. Use a piece of bent wire to secure the cut area down. Cover and firm the area with soil. Keep the soil moist and roots will develop in six to eight weeks. After rooting, sever the shoots close to both the layer and mother plant.*

It is not a quick way to produce new plants, often taking up to two years, but is easily done:
• Select a healthy, vigorous, low-growing stem or branch, one or two years old. Lower it to soil level and form a sloping trench, 7.5–15cm/3–6in deep at its lowest point and 23–45cm/9–18in from the shoot's tip.
• Lower the shoot into the depression and bend its tip upright. Either make a tongued cut at the point of the bend, or cut half-way around the stem and remove part of the bark.
• Use a wooden peg or piece of bent wire to hold the stem in the soil. Cover and firm with soil, then water.
• Tie the end of the stem to an upright cane.
• When young shoots develop from the shoot's tip, sever the stem and either plant into a nurserybed or a border.

LAYERING RIGID STEMS

Most stems are layered at ground-level. However, rigid stems that cannot be lowered are encouraged to form roots by wrapping sphagnum moss or peat around a purposely damaged part and enveloping it in polythene.

An earlier form of this method was used in China and India and known as Gootee-layering or Marcottage, but another way was to layer a shoot in the top of a large bamboo cane. A wide bamboo cane, about 1.5m/5ft long, was fixed in the ground. At its top, a 13cm/5in deep, 12–18mm/$^1/_2$–$^3/_4$in-wide slit was cut on one side and a 5cm/3in deep one on the other, to form an aerial pot.

Fine soil was packed in the bamboo's top, and the stem partly cut and inserted into the cane, with soil packed around it. Keeping the compost moist was essential to encourage roots.

INCREASE Holly by pegging down a branch in a trench in winter, but not immediately burying it. In spring, when shoots develop, regularly earth them up. Sever and pot up in autumn.

TIP layer blackberry and loganberry shoots in late summer. Peg down the tips with a large stone or U-shape wire. Cover and firm with soil. Shoots develop roots by late spring and can be severed. To make transplanting easier, peg shoots in pots of compost.

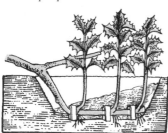

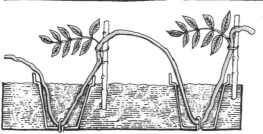

SERPENTINE layering produces several plants from one shoot and is ideal for increasing clematis and wisteria. Peg down a shoot at regular intervals into pots of well-drained compost.

LAYERING HOUSEPLANTS

❖

Layering long shoots of house-plants grown for their attrac-tive foliage and climbing or trailing nature is an exceptionally easy way to increase these plants.

Layering is a slow way to increase plants, but it is easy and does not need expensive or spe-cialised equipment.

Unlike when taking leaf-stem cuttings, where many new plants can be created from a single stem, a layered shoot will produce only one new plant. However, several long shoots from one mother plant can be layered at the same time.

Layering performed indoors cre-ates a focus of interest for several months, and although a slow way of increasing plants it is a more certain method than by cuttings.

Late spring and early summer are the best times to layer house-plants, when they are growing strongly. Rooted layers produced from them are then able to become fully established before the onset of winter and relatively poor light conditions.

EQUIPMENT REQUIRED

All that is needed is a few 7.5cm/3in-wide pots, a mixture of equal parts moist peat and sharp sand, bent pieces of wire, scissors or a sharp knife.

It is also useful to have a large plastic tray in which the mother plant and pots of layered shoots can be stood while forming roots. This makes moving them easier than if they are all separate.

The day before forming the lay-ers, water the mother plant several times to ensure its stems are fully charged with water. Dry shoots are difficult to bend without breaking and they do not readily develop roots.

Select a healthy shoot and bend it 10–15cm/4–6in from its tip. This constricts the flow of sap and thereby encourages the develop-ment of new roots.

1. SELECT *a healthy, relatively young ivy shoot – still attached to the parent plant – and bend it near to a leaf joint, 10–15cm/ 4–6in from its tip. This constricts the flow of sap and encourages the rapid development of roots.*

2. USE *a U-shaped wire to secure the bent part in a small pot of equal parts moist peat and sharp sand firmed to 12mm/$1/2$in of the rim. Water to settle com-post around the stem. Place the mother plant and layer in a plastic tray.*

3. KEEP *the compost moist and when young growths start to appear from the shoot's tip, sever the layer from the mother plant. Use sharp scissors and cut close to the new plant. Also cut the stem near to the mother plant's base.*

Fill and firm a pot with equal parts of moist peat and sharp sand to within 12mm/$^{1}/_{2}$in of its rim. Position the pot near the bend and pin it into the compost with a piece of bent wire. Firm compost over and around it, then water.

If the end of the shoot flops over and tends to loosen the layer in the compost, use a thin, short split-cane to hold it up.

AFTERCARE

Until roots develop, keep the mother plant well watered, as well as the compost in the small pots con taining the layers.

Place the mother plant and layers in good light and gentle warmth. Unlike cuttings, which are formed from severed pieces of plants and therefore cannot normally be exposed to high temperatures, layered shoots can be given their normal temperatures and occupy the same positions.

After several weeks, new shoots develop from the tips of shoots. This is a clue to the formation of roots. Remove the bent wire and gently tug the stem. If it resists being pulled up, this is an indication that roots have formed.

Sever the stem close to the new plant's base. Also, tidy up the stem by cutting it back to the mother plant's base.

ESTABLISHED PLANTS

After newly-rooted houseplants have been severed from their parents, they can be displayed indoors. Unfortunately, as each plant has only one stem, its initial display, when compared with established plants raised from cuttings and where several are put into the same pot, is not so eye-catching. However, when used to trail from wall-brackets or the tops of high shelves or bookcases they are equally as attractive.

LAYERING A SWEETHEART PLANT

ALSO *known as Heart-leaf,* Philodendron scandens *develops heart-shaped leaves on trailing or climbing stems. Pin a stem into a pot of moist peat and sharp sand.*

When young shoots grow from the shoot's tip, sever the stem close to the new plant. Also, tidy up the mother plant by cutting the stem close to its base.

HOUSEPLANTS RAISED FROM LAYERED SHOOTS

- Canary Island Ivy (*Hedera canariensis* 'Gloire de Marengo')
- English Ivy (*Hedera helix* – and its wide range of varieties)
- Grape Ivy (*Cissus rhombifolia*)
- Kangaroo Vine (*Cissus antarctica*)
- Swedish Ivy (*Plectranthus coleoides* 'Marginatus')
- Sweetheart Plant/Heart-leaf (*Philodendron scandens*)
- Wax Ivy/Cape Ivy (*Senecio macroglossus* 'Variegatus')

AIR LAYERING

THIS is a fascinating way to increase plants and is especially suitable for those growing indoors, in sun-rooms and greenhouses.

Many large, long-lived houseplants lose their lower leaves, and although still attractive towards their tops, appear bare and disfigured at their bases. Instead of having to throw them away, they can be air layered, lowered and given a new span of life.

Candidates for air layering must be healthy and with at least 45cm/1¹/2ft of stem at their tops packed with leaves. Although this technique can be performed throughout the year, it is more successful from spring to late summer when growth is strong.

TECHNIQUE OF AIR LAYERING

Using a sharp knife, make an upward-slanting cut about two-thirds through the stem and 7.5–10cm/3–4in below the lowest leaf. At this stage, take care that the upper part does not snap off.

Wedge open the cut, using a matchstick, and dust the cut surfaces with hormone rooting-powder. Push it well inside the cut.

Wind a piece of polythene around the stem and secure it 5cm/2in below the cut. Pack moist peat or sphagnum moss into it and tie a similar distance above the injury.

AFTERCARE

Keep the compost moist and the plant in gentle warmth. Within six to eight weeks, roots develop from the cut and can be seen through the polythene.

Sever the stem below the peat and pot up into a clean pot. Until established, support with a cane.

Cut the old, leafless plant down to 15–23cm/6–9in high and just above a bud. Keep the compost moist and young shoots will soon develop. If a bushy plant is desired, leave all shoots intact, but to produce a single stem remove all but one shoot.

PLANTS INCREASED BY AIR LAYERING

- Dracaena
- Dumb Cane (*Dieffenbachia*)
- Rubber Plant (*Ficus elastica* – and its many varieties)
- Swiss Cheese Plant (*Monstera deliciosa*)

GOOTEE-LAYERING

Also known as Marcottage, this form of encouraging stems to develop roots was practised in China and India in early times.

It was originated to propagate trees too difficult to increase by cuttings but which could be raised from layers. Normally, layers are encouraged to root in soil at ground level, but with Gootee-layering a stem is cut immediately under a leaf-bud or node with a slanting cut upwards and a stone or small piece of stick placed in it.

Around this was packed a ball of sticky soil, then covered with coir fibre or moss. Because Gootee-layering was used before polythene was available to retain moisture around the stem, a source of dampness was provided by a bamboo bucket suspended above it and a wick employed to transfer water.

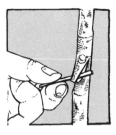

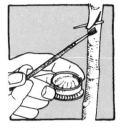

1. AIR *layer a Rubber Plant by using a sharp knife to make an upward-slanting cut, two-thirds through the stem and 7.5-10cm/3-4in below the lowest leaf.*

2. USE *a matchstick to keep the cut open. At this stage, latex (sticky, white sap) will exude from the cut: wipe this away with a damp cloth.*

3. DUST *the cut surfaces with a hormone rooting-powder. Use a small brush and push powder well inside the cut. Cut off the ends of very long matchsticks.*

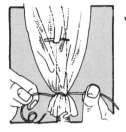

4. WIND *a piece of strong, clear polythene film – about 30cm/12in long by 25cm/10in wide – around the stem. Tie it about 5cm/2in below the cut.*

5. FILL *the tube formed by the polythene with moist peat or sphagnum moss. It is essential to pack it firmly around the stem and to about 5cm/2in above the cut.*

6. TIE *the polythene around the stem, firmly but not so tight that it restricts growth. If excessive polythene is left above and below the string, this can be trimmed back.*

7. KEEP *the potting compost in the mother plant's pot moist, and within six to eight weeks roots will appear inside the polythene. Use sharp secateurs or a knife to carefully sever the stem below the peat.*

8. REMOVE *the polythene. Pot up the plant immediately, retaining as much peat or sphagnum moss as possible, before the roots dry out. Until established, support the plant with a stake.*

Rubber Plant (Ficus elastica)

RUNNERS

❖

ENCOURAGING runners to grow roots is an easy and assured way to increase the sort of plants that develop plantlets at the ends of long stems.

In nature, plantlets on the ends of runners normally rest on the soil, and eventually roots develop from them to form new plants.

A few plants that are grown as houseplants also produce runners, and are easily increased by pegging them in small pots of equal parts moist peat and sharp sand. It can be done at any time of the year, but spring and summer are the best as the plants are then growing strongly.

Spider Plants are dramatic and eye-catching, especially when displayed in indoor hanging-baskets or on pedestals.

WATER THOROUGHLY

Water the mother plant the day before pinning down the plantlets.

Place several small pots around the mother plant and use small pieces of U-shaped wire to secure each plantlet.

Place the mother plant and small pots in a large plastic tray: this enables all the plants to be moved at the same time without any risk of plantlets being dislodged. It also ensures that when they are watered, excess moisture does not create problems. At this stage, each plantlet is still attached to the mother plant.

Rooting is indicated when plantlets develop fresh shoots and leaves. Use sharp scissors to cut the runner, close to the plantlet as well as at the mother plant's base.

Place the young plants in gentle warmth and light shade until established and growing strongly.

Silvery veins above, flushed red beneath

Thin, wiry stems

Strawberry Geraniums (Saxifraga stolonifera)

Young plants

STRAWBERRY GERANIUMS

Few trailing houseplants are as popular and widely grown as this stunningly attractive East Asian plant. In warm regions it is also placed outdoors during summer.

Also known as Mother-of-Thousands, it has roundish, somewhat heart-shaped leaves. Runners, often 90cm/3ft or more long, bear young plants that can be encouraged to form roots. The form 'Tricolor', widely known as Magic Carpet, has leaves variegated in pink and pale yellow.

Spider Plants are easily increased by pinning down young plantlets that develop at the ends of long, white, arching stems into compost in small pots. Several new plants can be raised at one time from a single mother plant. Stand all the plants in a plastic tray – it makes handling them much easier.

1. POSITION *small pots containing equal parts moist peat and sharp sand around a mother plant, so that plantlets can be easily pinned into them.*

2. USE *bent pieces of wire to secure each plantlet in a small pot. Firm compost around the plantlets. Water the compost lightly but thoroughly.*

3. WHEN *the plantlets develop roots and fresh shoots, sever each stem close to its plantlet. Also, cut it off right at the base of the mother plant.*

INCREASING STRAWBERRIES

Plants of this popular fruit are easily increased by pegging down runners in small pots.

During early and mid-summer, select runners on one-year-old, healthy, disease-free plants and use pieces of U-shaped wire to peg them down in 7.5cm/3in-wide pots of compost. Bury these small pots to their rims in soil around the mother plant.

Do not layer more than five runners from any plant; remove all others.

Keep the compost moist and remove all flowers.

When the runners have developed roots – six to eight weeks later – sever the stems and plant into a fruit garden.

STRAWBERRIES RUNNERS IN TUBS

Strawberry plants are ideal for planting in a large barrel, where they fruit ten to fourteen days before those at ground-level.
- *Drill drainage holes in the tub's base. Stand it on bricks.*
- *Drill 6–7.5cm/2$\frac{1}{2}$–3in holes, 15–20cm/6–8in apart, in its sides.*
- *Insert a 15cm/6in wide, wire-netting tube in the barrel's centre. Fill with clean rubble.*
- *Fill around the drainage tube with compost, at the same time setting a plant in in each hole.*
- *Set several plants at the top and lightly water.*

PLANTLETS

◆

A few plants develop plantlets on their leaves and thereby provide a fascinating way to increase them – one with special appeal to children.

Few ways of increasing plants are as easy as rooting plantlets. Some plants, such as the Chandelier Plant and Devil's Backbone, have plantlets that can be removed and pressed on moist compost. Others, like the Hen-and-Chicken Plant and Pig-a-Back Plant, have leaves with plantlets on their upper surfaces. These are laid flat on moist compost and pegged in position.

Early and mid-summer are the best times to propagate these amusing and fascinating plants.

PLANTS INCREASED
FROM PLANTLETS

- Chandelier Plant (*Kalanchoe tubiflora/Bryophyllum tubiflorum*)
- Devil's Backbone (*Kalanchoe daigremontiana/Bryophyllum daigremontianum*)
- Hen-and-chicken Plant (*Asplenium bulbiferum*)
- Pig-a-back Plant (*Tolmiea menziesii*)

HEN-AND-CHICKEN PLANT
Also known as Mother Fern, the Australian and New Zealand Asplenium bulbiferum has finely-cut, mid-green, feathery fronds that when mature develop small plantlets known as bulbils on their upper surfaces.

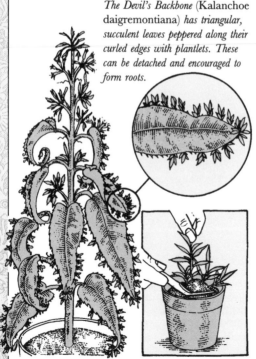

The Devil's Backbone (Kalanchoe daigremontiana) *has triangular, succulent leaves peppered along their curled edges with plantlets. These can be detached and encouraged to form roots.*

1. DETACH *mature plantlets and press (above) on the surface of equal parts moist peat and sharp sand. Water lightly to settle the compost around them.*

2. PLACE *in light shade and gentle warmth and keep the compost lightly moist. When rooted and about 2.5cm/1in high (left), transfer the plantlets into small, individual pots. Use a small dibber to form a hole, hold the rooted plantlet in it and lever compost around the roots to hold them firmly.*

EASY FOR CHILDREN

The Chandelier Plant (Kalanchoe tubiflora) *grows to about 90cm/3ft high and produces groups of plantlets at the ends of succulent, cylindrical leaves.*

The plantlets naturally fall off plants and when sprinkled on moist compost soon develop roots. They root rapidly and when about 2.5cm/1in long are potted up, setting three in a 7.5cm/3in-wide pot. Each stem is then able to offer slight support to its neighbour.

In spring, plants develop a crown of small orange, bell-like flowers.

In nature, these bulbils gradually weigh down fronds, and on reaching the ground develop roots and create more plants. These bulbils, however, can be removed, pressed into moist compost and encouraged to form roots.

Fill a large tray or box with equal parts moist peat and sharp sand. Detach a mature leaf and press it on the compost. Either place small stones on the frond, or secure with pieces of bent wire.

Keep the compost moist, place in gentle warmth and light shade. The bulbils develop roots and are potted up individually.

PIG-A-BACK PLANT

Variously known as Young-on-Age, Pickaback, Piggyback Plant and Thousand Mothers, *Tolmiea menziesii* is native to and grows wild in the western states of North America. It develops small plantlets on the upper surfaces of its maple-like, 10cm/4in-wide, dull green leaves.

It is easy to grow and survives in cool rooms and low light.

Detach leaves with plantlets and place on moist compost in a seed-tray. Use U-shaped pieces of wire to secure the leaf. Place in gentle warmth and light shade.

The plantlets soon develop roots and when established are potted up into 7.5cm/3in pots. Later, transfer into a larger pot.

TROPICAL PROPAGATION PITS

In tropical regions, high temperatures and strong sunlight are a problem and likely to desiccate cuttings before they have a chance to develop roots.

Earlier, propagation pits were an answer to this problem, creating cool and shaded areas. Pits about 90cm/3ft deep were dug in sheltered places and covered with palm leaves. A layer of sand in the pit's base created a cool and well-drained base for pots of cuttings, although it needed to be kept damp.

At high elevations in India, permanent pits were dug and given glass-covered roofs. If warmth at the bases of cuttings was required, the bottom of the pit was filled with fermenting horse dung and then covered with a layer of fine soil.

In some areas, protection from wind and rain was also needed and often provided by a thatched roof, 1.2m/4ft at its back and 1.8m/6ft at the front, and facing the morning sun.

SUCKERS

❦ NCREASING plants by removing shoots that arise from their roots is an easy way to propagate them. Indeed, it is a method well-known to Mother Nature and therefore man's involvement is only to sever suckers and to plant them in a border or nurserybed.

Only plants growing on their own roots can be increased in this way. Those that are grafted or budded are not suitable, as in such cases only the root part – and not the desired varietal element – would be increased.

SIMILAR TO DIVISION AND LAYERING

Increasing plants by suckers is, of course, closely related to several other forms of propagation.

When dividing fibrous-rooted herbaceous plants the roots are separated, while some layers run underground and often appear a step away from the parent plant.

Suckers, however, are where the plant's own inclinations are to

> ### RICH AUTUMN COLOURS
>
> *Few shrubs are as attractive in autumn as the Staghorn Sumach* (Rhus typhina), *which is easily increased from suckers.*
> *Its large, mid-green leaves, formed of many leaflets, assume rich orange-scarlet tints.*

send up a shoots from its roots, as a natural way to increase itself.

Remove suckers in autumn or spring. Where plants have produced suckers, these are removed by digging down around the young shoots and, with a sharp knife, severing them. Leave as much fibrous root attached to them as possible.

Much of the soil around a sucker is usually disturbed and falls off. Cut away old woody parts, damaged stems or weak and small shoots, so that a healthy plant remains.

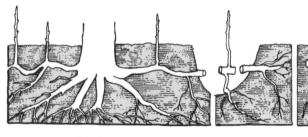

1. MANY *trees and shrubs naturally send up shoots from their roots. The roots of some shrubs, if damaged during normal soil cultivation such as digging, are further encouraged to produce suckers, which inevitably create a jungle of shoots on the surface.*

2. IN *autumn or spring, dig down to the roots and use a sharp knife to cut away suckers. Young, healthy shoots are the best ones to take to form new plants. Older ones can be used but cut away woody and damaged parts. Do not cut off fibrous roots.*

3. SUCKERS *are usually large enough to be planted directly in a border. However, if the new border is not ready, temporarily plant them in trenches to keep their roots damp. Alternatively, wrap them in moist hessian and place in a cool shed.*

RAISING TROPICAL FRUITS FROM SUCKERS

Several tropical fruits are increased from suckers, providing an easy way to propagate them, especially in warm, moist areas.

There are two types of suckers used to increase these fruits:

pineapple

• *Root-suckers arise from buds on the roots and include such plants as Breadfruit and bananas.*

New plants can be created by severing suckers from the parent plant and removing them with a large number of roots attached.

banana

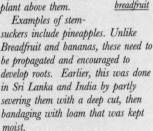

• *Stem-suckers (also known as ratoons) spring from the bases of stems. They are also called 'gourmandisers', as they usually grow at the expense of the part of the plant above them.*

breadfruit

Examples of stem-suckers include pineapples. Unlike Breadfruit and bananas, these need to be propagated and encouraged to develop roots. Earlier, this was done in Sri Lanka and India by partly severing them with a deep cut, then bandaging with loam that was kept moist.

Plants that have been severely pruned develop stem-suckers.

Replant it before the roots become dry. If planting is delayed, dig a small trench in an out-of-the-way position and bury the roots, firming moist soil over them. For short periods, however, wrap the roots in damp sacking and place in a cool, vermin-proof shed. Position out of direct sun.

Like all new plants, firm planting is essential as roots must be in close contact with the soil if they are to become established quickly. Pockets of air delay their development as they encourage fibrous roots to dry, harden and eventually become useless to the plant. Use the heel of your shoe to ensure firm planting.

PLANTS INCREASED
FROM SUCKERS
• False Castor Oil Plant/Japanese Aralia (*Fatsia japonica*)
• Popular (*Populus*)
• Smooth Sumach (*Rhus glabra*)
• Staghorn Sumach (*Rhus typhina*)

THE POISONOUS SUMACHS

*Sumachs are easily increased from suckers, but are among the most poisonous of all shrubs and trees. The Poison Sumach (*Rhus vernix*), native to swamplands of North America, has stems that are poisonous to touch.*

*The closely-related Varnish Tree (*Rhus verniciflua*) is also poisonous, but has the redeeming characteristic in that varnish is extracted from lacerations in its bark. The liquid is collected and allowed to oxidize in air, when it becomes black and hard. This rhus also produces an oil used to make candles.*

*The Poison Ivy of North America has a very appropriate botanical name, *Rhus toxicodendron*. The stems are considered by many Indian tribes to be poisonous.*

GRAFTING TO
CREATE NEW PLANTS

❖

 WHEN grafts are made to create new plants, there are always two distinct parts: the root section and the variety.

WHIP AND
TONGUE GRAFTING

Widely used to create new fruit trees such as apples and pears, this method appears complex because of the tongue, but is actually easy to prepare.

Grafting is performed at the end of the dormant season. Cut down the root part (stock) to 7.5–10cm/3–4in above the ground. Use a sharp knife to create a 36mm/1¹/₂in-long sloping cut. Half-way down the slant, make a cut in a downward direction. This forms one of the tongues.

Prepare the varietal (scion) part from a healthy, one-year-old shoot. Cut the top slightly above a healthy bud and the base fractionally under the third or fourth bud below it. On the side opposite the lowest bud, form a slanting cut 36mm/1¹/₂in long. Half way along the slope, make an upward cut. This forms the other tongue.

Gently push the tongue on the scion into the tongue of the stock. Do not force them: it may be necessary to increase one cut.

When the scion and stock are the same diameter they usually fit together easily. However, if the scion is much smaller, ensure that instead of being positioned in the centre, the edges are aligned on one side. This is to ensure that the cambium (inner bark) layers unite.

Tie raffia around the graft and cover with grafting wax. Additionally, put a blob of wax on the top of the scion. Remove the wax and raffia as soon as growth commences.

  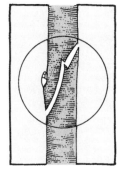 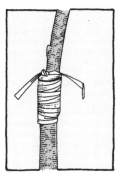

1. WHIP *and tongue grafting is widely used to produce fruit and ornamental trees. The varietal part (scion) is formed of a shoot three or four buds. Form a slanting cut, 36mm/1¹/₂in long, on the side opposite the lowest bud.*

2. CUT *the root part (stock) 7.5–10cm/3–4in above the ground and make a 36mm/1¹/₂in long slanting cut. Use a sharp knife to cut a 'tongue' in the stock and scion, so that they will lock together and hold the scion part secure.*

3. BIND *raffia around the graft and cover with grafting wax to make it waterproof. The edges of the stock and scion should be in contact, as this is where they initially unite. Place a small piece of wax on the top of the scion to seal it.*

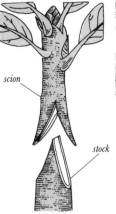

scion

stock

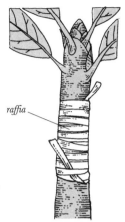

raffia

1. SADDLE *grafting is frequently used to propagate named varieties of rhododendrons. It is usually performed in gentle warmth in a greenhouse, in late winter or early spring.*

2. CUT *the root part (stock) 5-7.5cm/2-3in high and use a sharp knife to create an inverted V-shape. Cut the scion to fit and position on top of the stock. Tie quickly with one piece of raffia.*

3. USE *raffia to secure the stock and scion. It is not necessary to cover the grafted area with wax, as the plant is left in a greenhouse and moisture can be kept off the grafted area.*

SADDLE GRAFTING

Like its name indicates, this graft resembles a saddle-like stock, with the varietal part sitting on top.

Unlike whip and tongue grafts, it does not have a special device to keep the scion fixed to the stock. This is because saddle grafting is mainly performed in a greenhouse and special care can be taken to ensure the two parts are not knocked and separated.

Saddle grafting is performed in late winter or early spring. It is mainly used to propagate rhododendrons

The first stage is to cut the root part 5–7.5cm/2–3in high and to create an inverted V-shape. Cut the scion to fit and position on top of the stock. Use raffia to secure them together. It is not necessary to cover the grafted area with wax, as moisture can be kept off the area in a greenhouse.

If the scion is smaller than the stock, ensure they unite on one of the sides. Preferably, the size of the scion should match the width of the root-stock. Do not leave the saddle in the middle of the stock. To reduce the amount of moisture needed to keep the scion part healthy, cut about a third off the ends of large leaves.

APPROACH GRAFTING *was popular in the nineteenth century to increase fruit trees.*

The root-stock was grown in a pot and positioned near the desired variety, grafted and later severed.

REJUVENATING OLD FRUIT TREES

❖

 IN EARLIER years it was common to see apple trees 6m/20ft or more high, crowned in late summer with fruits too high to be picked. If such trees are inherited in a garden the choice is either to dig them out or to rejuvenate them by grafting new varieties on the branches.

TOPWORKING

This is when the branch system is cut off 60–90cm/2–3ft above the crotch and a completely new branch system formed.

There are several grafts used in topworking, but the easiest one to master is rind grafting, also known as crown or cleft grafting, and illustrated below.

Cut off the main branches any time during winter. In mid-spring, when the sap is starting to flow, prepare the varietal parts (scions), cutting slightly above a bud and just above the fourth or fifth bud below it. Then, at its lower end, make a sloping cut about 36mm/1¹⁄₂in long on the side opposite the lowest bud.

Prepare the tree by cutting the branches back slightly and smoothing the wood. Use a sharp knife to make two or three cuts vertically and 2.5–5cm/1–2in long down the sides of each branch. If the rind does not lift easily, use a thin spatula to start it. Then, insert a scion into each slit.

Bind the branch with soft string or raffia and cover with grafting

TOPWORKING

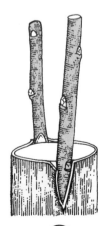

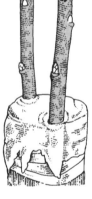

2. CUT *the main branches to within 60–90cm/2–3ft of the crotch. Make two or three, 2.5–5cm/1–2in-long cuts down the stub's side and push a varietal part firmly into each one.*

1. RIND *grafting is a way to rejuvenate old apple trees. Prepare the varietal part by cutting above its top, and just above the forth or fifth bud below it, making a slanting cut.*

3. TIGHTLY *wrap raffia or soft string around the branch, to secure the scions (varietal parts) and cover with grafting wax. Additionally, cover the cut tops of the scions with wax.*

FRAMEWORK GROWTH

STUB GRAFTING *involves partly severing a shoot and inserting a scion. The branch is then cut off and tension secures the scion in the slit (top).*

SIDE GRAFTING *involves cutting a branch, inserting a scion and positioning it at the cut's side. The tension of the cut holds the scions in place.*

INVERTED-L GRAFTING *is when an L-shaped cut is made in the rind and a scion inserted in it. Secure with a small nail and cover with wax.*

wax. In summer, when the scions start to grow, cut the binding to prevent it constricting growth.

FRAMEWORK GRAFTING

This is less radical than topworking, and involves leaving the tree's main branches in place and replacing the side branches. Framework grafting takes longer than topworking, but there is less risk of diseases entering large cuts and the tree is returned to cropping much quicker.

The range of framework grafts is wide and interesting: stub, side and inverted-L grafting are three of many. Each of these types of graft is illustrated above.

• Stub grafting uses the tension in a shoot to hold the graft secure. A cut is made close to a branch, a scion inserted and the shoot severed. Cover the bare surfaces with grafting wax.

• Side grafting is performed on a main branch to produce a sideshoot. Make a shallow cut and insert a scion at an angle, so that it aligns with one of the cut's sides. Cover with wax.

• Inverted-L grafts also create sideshoots. Secure the graft with a small nail and cover with wax.

GRAFTING IN TUDOR TIMES

Gardeners during the fifteenth and sixteenth centuries knew about grafting trees and frequently used a technique we now know as cleft grafting.

A vertical slit was cut in the bark and the scion (varietal part) inserted in it.

The scions were bound and covered with a paste, created from mud, straw, dung and water, to prevent drying out.

BUDDING

❖

T HE technique of budding very much resembles grafting, but involves uniting only one bud with each rootstock. It is also a quicker method and, commercially, is much more economic as less buds are needed.

The vast majority of roses are raised by budding. This is when a bud of the varietal part is united with the rootstock.

Budding is also used to increase many ornamental trees and shrubs, including crab apples, but its main value is to raise new rose bushes each year.

BUDDING ROSES
Bush roses are budded 36–50mm/ 1¹/2–2in above the ground.

Successful budding depends on the rind lifting easily from the wood and therefore mid-summer is the best time. Prepare the varietal part in the way shown below.

For bush roses, initially scrape away soil from the rootstock's base. In hot areas, make the T-cut on the side most protected from strong sunlight; in others, the side towards the prevailing wind is best as the bud is not then easily blown off. Insert the bud as indicated below, severing the raffia later.

The technique of budding standard roses is exactly the same as for bush types. The only difference is that three buds are used and inserted well above the ground: 75–90cm/ 2¹/2–3ft for half-standards and 1.2–1.3m/ 4–4¹/2ft for full standards. Root-stocks are prepared by allowing a single stem to grow well above the desired height and supporting it with a stake.

1. BUDDING *is the main way to raise roses. Select a shoot with young, plump buds and cut off the leaves, leaving stalks 12mm/¹/2in long. Insert a sharp knife 18mm/³/4in above the bud and, passing under it, emerge 12mm/¹/2in below it so that the bud is cut off.*

2. SCRAPE *away loose soil from around the root-stock and 36–50mm/1¹/2–2in above the ground, make a T-shaped cut. The vertical cut is about 36mm/1¹/2in long and the horizontal one 12–18mm/¹/2–³/4in. Use the spatula end of a budding knife to lift the rind.*

3. HOLD *the bud by its leaf-stalk and insert into the T-cut. It may be necessary again to use the spatula end of a budding knife to open the flaps. When it is securely in the T-cut, use a sharp knife to carefully cut off any woody part that may be protruding above it.*

In late autumn or early winter, sever it about 15cm/6in above the desired height and in spring allow three shoots to develop from the head. Rub off buds lower down.

In mid-summer, insert three buds into the shoots, on their upper surfaces and close to the main stem. Later, cut off the stems about 2.5cm/1in beyond the buds, as well as cutting the main stem slightly above the uppermost shoot.

The above applies when using briar roses (*Rosa canina*), whereas with rugosa (*Rosa rugosa*) types the buds are inserted directly into the plant's main stem.

Until the buds develop and produce shoots, sucker-like growths are frequently a problem on the stems of standard roses. If seen early, they can be easily removed by just rubbing them sideways. If left, they attempt to dominate the plant and their removal often initiates the development of further suckers on the main stem. Also, remove suckers from the roots.

ROOTSTOCKS FOR ROSES

Several types of rose species are used to create the root parts of roses, although some, such as miniature roses, are raised from cuttings.

• *Seedling Briar* (Rosa canina): *Raised from seeds and more than 80% of all roses are budded on it. They are long-lived and with deep roots, ideal for medium and heavy soils but not light and sandy types.*

• *Cutting Briar* (Rosa canina): *Raised from cuttings and ideal on medium soils. Not now widely used but good for standard and half-standard forms, as well as weeping roses.*

• *Rugosa* (Rosa rugosa): *Raised from cuttings and develop a large, coarse root system. Does not live as long as briar types. Plants are ideal as stocks for standard and half-standard forms.*

4. SECURE *the bud firmly in position either with raffia or a proprietary budding tie. When using raffia, first make it pliable by immersing in water for a few minutes. Ensure that the bud is not covered and that the leaf stalk is not knocked or damaged in any way.*

5. SUCCESSFUL *budding becomes apparent three to four weeks later: the bud will appear plump and the leaf stalk drops off. At this stage, use a sharp knife to cut the raffia on the side opposite the bud. If left, it constricts growth by cutting off sap flow.*

6. USE *sharp secateurs to cut off the part of the root-stock 12mm/1/2in above the budded position in early or mid-spring of the following year. At the same time, cut off, as close as possible to their point of origin, any sucker shoots growing from the root-stock.*

PROPAGATION CALENDAR

SPRING

This is the main season of birth and regeneration, especially for plants raised from seeds. There are many propagation jobs to be tackled both in greenhouses and gardens, although outdoors the main influencing factor is the weather; some areas are free of frost in early spring, while others as late as early summer. Do not risk sowing or planting tender plants outdoors too early as they will be killed by frost. Young shoots on seedlings as well as dahlias are very susceptible to low temperatures.

IN THE GREENHOUSE
- Air layering (46–47)
- Cacti and other succulents from cuttings (34–35)
- Cane cuttings (32–33)
- Cross-sections of leaves (30–31)
- Dividing houseplants (40–41)
- Layering houseplants (44–45)
- Leaf cuttings (26–31)
- Leaf-petiole cuttings (25)
- Leaf-stem cuttings (24)
- Leaf-square cuttings (28–29)
- Leaf-triangle cuttings (28–29)
- Plantlets on houseplants (50–51)
- Runners on houseplants (48–49)
- Soft-wood cuttings, such as dahlias and chrysanthemums (18–19)
- Sowing half-hardy annuals (10–11)
- Whole-leaf cuttings (26–27)

IN THE GARDEN
- Dividing dahlia tubers (38–39)
- Dividing herbaceous plants (36–37)
- Grafting (54–57)
- Layering shrubs (42–43)
- Suckers (52–53)
- Sowing hardy annuals (12–13)
- Sowing vegetable seeds (16–17)

SUMMER

Although many seeds can be sown and cuttings taken during early summer, by mid-summer some greenhouses are given over to growing tomatoes, cucumbers or melons. In gardens, seeds of many vegetables are still sown up to early summer, as well as quick maturing salad crops until mid-summer. During the early part of summer, seeds of herbaceous perennials are sown to raise plants that can be planted out into a border in autumn or spring. Biennials are also raised about the same time, the plants flowering during the following spring and early summer. Some tasks, such as dividing rhizomatous irises, are best tackled after their flowers fade early summer, or later in the season during late summer. Many specialists prefer the earlier time.

IN THE GREENHOUSE
- Air layering (46–47)
- Cacti and other succulents from cuttings (34–35)
- Cane cuttings (32–33)
- Cross-sections of leaves (30–31)
- Dividing houseplants (40–41)
- Layering houseplants (44–45)
- Leaf-cuttings (26–31)
- Leaf-square cuttings (28–29)
- Leaf-stem cuttings (24)
- Leaf-triangle cuttings (28–29)
- Plantlets on houseplants (50–51)
- Runners on houseplants (48–49)
- Soft-wood cuttings (18–19)
- Whole-leaf cuttings (26–27)

IN THE GARDEN
- Budding (58–59)
- Dividing rhizomatous irises (38)
- Sowing hardy biennials (14–15)
- Sowing herbaceous perennials (14–15)
- Sowing vegetable seeds (16–17)

AUTUMN

In some regions and in a few years, early autumn can be just as hot as summer, but mostly it is a season when plants mature and indicate the closing of another year. It is, however, the season of hardwood cuttings, which shopuld be taken from shoots produced earlier in the year. And as leaves fall from deciduous shrubs it makes it easier to see which low-growing stems can be layered, an easy way for all gardeners to increase shrubs. Layering also has the advantage of not requiring any specialized propagation equipment, other than a knife.

IN THE GREENHOUSE

• Cut down outdoor chrysanthemums as they finish flowering and pack their roots (stools) in boxes of compost in readiness for producing cuttings during late winter and spring. Initially, place them in a cool, frost-proof position; later, move them into gentle warmth in a greenhouse in readiness for taking cuttings (18–19).
• Cut down dahlia plants as soon as their foliage has frosted. Stand the tubers upside down in a shed. Later, they are placed in boxes, put in a frost-proof position and encouraged to develop shoots that form cuttings (18–19).
• Make root cuttings (22–23)

IN THE GARDEN

• Dividing herbaceous plants (36–37)
• Hardwood cuttings (21) of a wide range of fruit bushes, such as blackcurrants, gooseberries and red and white currants.
• Hardwood cuttings of many ornamental flowering shrubs and hedging plants, such as Privet (21)
• Layering shrubs (42–43)
• Suckers (52–53)

WINTER

Apart from generally clearing up a garden in early winter and ensuring that all rubbish is taken away, the greenhouse will need attention. If it is empty – or the plants can be temporarily placed elsewhere – open up all doors and ventilators so that the cleansing action of the frost invades it. Also, scrub down the structure to ensure it is free from pests and diseases. Unless the greenhouse is clean, there is always the risk of cuttings and seedlings being attacked and killed. Also, check all heating and electrical equipment in readiness for the season of rebirth in late winter and early spring.

In conservatories and sunrooms – as well as some greenhouses – the temperature is kept relatively high to ensure tender houseplants do not die. Some of these, such as the Lollipop Plant *(Pachystachys lutea)*, can be cut down in mid-winter to encourage the development of shoots that will provide soft-wood cuttings in spring.

Order seeds well in advance of spring so that you are not disappointed later – the best and unusual varieties are always in demand and seed companies soon sell out of them.

IN THE GREENHOUSE

• Sowing seeds in late winter (10–11)
• Root cuttings (22–23)
• Saddle grafting (55)

IN THE GARDEN

• Grafting (54–57)
• Hardwood cuttings (21) of a wide range of fruit bushes, such as blackcurrants, gooseberries and red and white currants.
• Hardwood cuttings of shrubs and hedging plants, such as Privet (21)
• Layering shrubs (42–43)

USEFUL
PROPAGATION TERMS
❖

AIR LAYERING: *A method of encouraging roots to form on a stem.*

ANNUAL: *A plant that grows from seed, flowers and dies within the same year.*

ANTHER: *The male part of a flower that produces pollen.*

ASEXUAL: *Non-sexual; frequently used to refer to the propagation of plants by cuttings and other vegetative methods, including division.*

BIENNIAL: *A plant that makes its initial growth one year and flowers the following one, then dying.*

BIGENERIC HYBRID: *A plant produced by crossing two plants from different genera.*

BOTTOM HEAT: *The warming of a rooting mixture from below.*

BUDDING: *Uniting a bud of a varietal part with a root-stock of known vigour and quality.*

BULBIL: *A small, immature bulb found on the bases of some bulbs. They can be detached, sown and encouraged to form roots*

CAMBIUM: *Tissue just beneath the bark of woody plants. When grafting, the cambium of both parts must unite.*

CANE CUTTINGS: *Stems (without leaves) severed from a parent plant and either inserted vertically into compost or pressed on the surface.*

CLONE: *A plant raised vegetatively from another, and therefore identical to it.*

COMPOST: *Refers to the mixture in which cuttings are inserted, seeds sown and plants replanted. Can also refer to decomposed vegetative material.*

CUTTING: *A method of vegetative propagation, by which a severed part is encouraged to form roots.*

DIBBER: *Pencil-like, blunt-ended stick used to insert cuttings or transplant seedlings.*

DIVISION: *A vegetative method of propagation, involving dividing roots.*

EYE: *A growth bud on a tuber, or a bud on a stem.*

EYE CUTTINGS: *A method of increasing grape-vines.*

F1: *The first filial generation, the result of a cross between two pure-bred parents.*

FERTILIZATION: *The sexual union of the male cell with the female cell.*

FLUID SOWING: *Mixing seeds with a fluid gel, put in a flexible plastic tube and squeezed along a drill.*

GOOTEE-LAYERING: *Also known as Marcottage and used to encourage roots to develop on stems, usually shrubs and trees.*

GRAFTING: *The uniting of a varietal part with roots of known vigour.*

HALF-HARDY ANNUALS: *Plants raised in gentle warmth early in the year and later planted outdoors when the weather improves.*

HALF-RIPE CUTTINGS: *Formed of semi-ripe shoots.*

HARDENING OFF: *Slowly acclimatizing plants to outdoor conditions.*

HARDY ANNUALS: *Plants sown directly into their flowering positions out-doors.*

HEEL CUTTINGS: *A cutting, usually a semi-hardwood type, with part of a shoot attached to its base.*

HORMONE: *A chemical that influences the growth and development of plants. Often used to encourage root formation.*

HYBRID: *The progeny from parents of different species or genera.*

INTERNODE: *The length of stem between two leaf joints (nodes).*

INVERTED L-GRAFTING: *Graft used to rejuvenate old fruit trees.*

LAYERING: *Encouraging stems to develop roots, either in a greenhouse or garden.*

LEAF-PETIOLE CUTTINGS: *Formed of a leaf and its leaf stem.*

LEAF SQUARES: *Cutting a leaf into small squares that can be encouraged to form roots.*

LEAF-STEM CUTTINGS: *Formed of a piece of stem and a leaf.*

LEAF TRIANGLES: *Cutting a leaf into small triangles that can be encouraged to form roots.*

MARCOTTAGE: *Also known as Gootee-layering and used to encourage the development of roots on stems, usually trees and shrubs.*

MIST PROPAGATION: *A method of regularly covering cuttings with a fine mist spray to keep them cool, reduce transpiration and encourage rapid rooting.*

NODE: *The point at which leaves, stems or sideshoots arise. It is usually slightly swollen.*

NICKING: *Using a sharp knife to shallow cut a seed's coat to encourage rapid germination.*

PETIOLE: *Another term for a leaf stem.*

PLANTLETS: *Small, immature plants that develop on leaves or at the ends of stems.*

POLLINATION: *The alighting of pollen (male part) on the stigma (female part) of a plant.*

PRICKING OFF: *The initial moving of seedlings from where they were sown into pots or seed-trays.*

PROPAGATION: *Increasing plants.*

PROPAGATORS: *Enclosed, plastic or glass-covered units in which seeds are encouraged to germinate and cuttings to root. Some are heated.*

RHIZOME: *Horizontal, creeping, underground stem which acts as a storage organ. Can be divided to produce further plants.*

RIND GRAFTING: *Used to rejuvenate old fruit trees.*

ROOT CUTTINGS: *Ways to increase plants by severing roots and placing them in compost.*

ROOT-STOCK: *The roots upon which plants are grafted or budded.*

RUNNER: *A shoot that grows along the ground, rooting and forming new plants.*

SADDLE GRAFTING: *A method of grafting plants, especially rhododendrons.*

SCION: *A shoot or bud that is grafted on a root-stock.*

SEED-TRAY: *Flat-based tray in which seeds are sown and seedlings pricked off into. Known in North America as a flat.*

SEMI-HARDWOOD: *Another term for half-ripe cuttings.*

SEMI-MATURE: *Another term for half-ripe cuttings.*

SERPENTINE LAYERING: *Long stems when layered in loops.*

SIDE GRAFTING: *Used to rejuvenate old fruit trees.*

STIGMA: *The tip of the female reproductive organ on which pollen alights.*

STOOL: *Usually means the roots of cut-down chrysanthemums. Also refers to some shrubs with masses of shoots that grow from ground level.*

STRAIN: *Seed-raised plants from a common ancestor.*

STUB GRAFTING: *Used to rejuvenate old fruit trees by replacing side branches.*

STYLE: *Female part of a flower – links the stigma to the ovary.*

SUCKER: *A shoot that arises from below ground level, usually from roots but sometimes from stems.*

THINNING: *Removing congested seedlings to leave healthy ones spaced out.*

TI-LOG CUTTINGS: *Formed of stems (without leaves) and inserted into compost to encourage the formation of roots.*

TIP CUTTING: *A soft-wood cutting formed from a growing tip, piece of stem and few leaves.*

TIP LAYERING: *Encouraging tips of shoots to develop roots.*

TRANSPLANTING: *Moving young plants from a nurserybed to where they will grow and mature. The term is also used when established plants are moved.*

TUBER: *A thickened, fleshy root (dahlia) or an underground stem (potato). These can be increased by division.*

VEGETATIVE: *Refers to propagation and includes methods of increasing plants such as by cuttings, layers, grafting, budding and division. Sowing seeds is not a vegetative method.*

WHIP AND TONGUE GRAFTING: *Used to create some fruit trees.*

INDEX